Orders:
Box 20725
Birmingham, AL 35216

Editorial Address:
3601 Westbury Road
Birmingham, AL 35223

GEORGES PEREC
Traces of His Passage

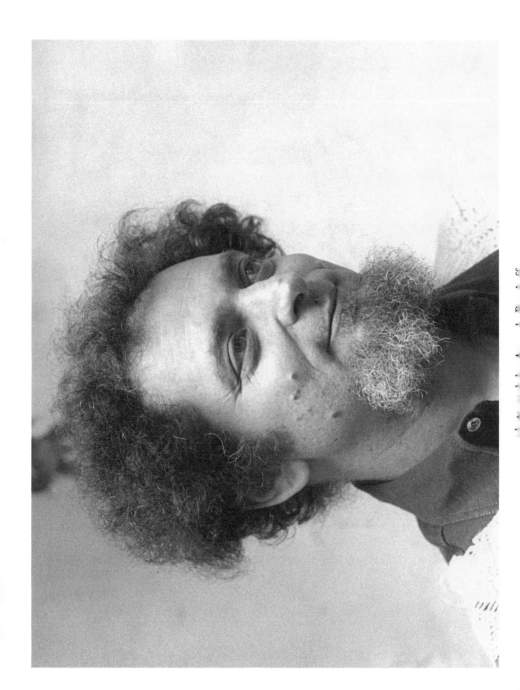

GEORGES PEREC
Traces of His Passage

by

Paul Schwartz

SUMMA PUBLICATIONS, INC.
Birmingham, Alabama
1988

Copyright 1988
Summa Publications, Inc.

ISBN 0-917786-60-2
Library of Congress Catalog Number 87-62927

Printed in the United States of America

For Lucy, Andrew, and Judson...

ACKNOWLEDGMENTS

I would like to express my gratitude to the University of North Dakota, especially to Dean Bernard O'Kelly and Vice-President Alice Clark, for granting me a year's leave to write this book. I am also grateful to friends in France who provided me with materials and information on Perec, especially Michel and Paul Veyret, and technical support, especially Michèle and Pierre Nieul, Steve Carroll, and Guy Daney. I thank Lucy Schwartz, Warren Motte, and David Bellos for their helpful reading of the manuscript. I thank the Association Georges Perec for its support and encouragement, and specifically Eric Beaumatin, Paulette Perec, and Bernard Magné for taking the time to respond to my tedious questions.

CONTENTS

INTRODUCTION

GEORGES PEREC'S BRIEF LITERARY CAREER IS REMARKABLY VARIED. In the span of fifteen years—1965 to 1980—he published seven novels, translations of two American novels, two collections of poetry, three books of nonfiction, numerous articles, a book of crossword puzzles, and a treatise on the game of *Go*. He also had two original plays performed, collaborated in the production of nine films,[1] and was cofounder of a sociological journal.[2]

Perec was born on March 7, 1936, the only son of Icek Judko Perec and Cyrla Szulewicz Perec, Jewish immigrants from Poland. Perec's father died in 1940 of wounds received defending France against the German invasion. His mother was arrested and deported in 1943 and died, presumably at Auschwitz. Young Perec spent the war years in Villard-de-Lans and Lans-en-Vercors in the French Alps and returned to Paris in 1945 with the family of his father's sister Esther Bienenfeld. He attended the Lycée Claude Bernard in Paris but finished his secondary education as a *pensionnaire* at the Collège d'Etampes, thirty miles south of Paris. On the faculty of the Collège was sociology professor Jean Duvignaud who became a lifelong mentor and friend.

Ten years later, Duvignaud reflects on his early impression of Perec:

> Voilà près de dix ans je vis entrer dans la classe de philosophie dont j'avais alors la responsabilité un jeune homme au sourire crispé et au regard traqué de jeune loup. Un pâle surveillant me dit qu'il s'agissait d'un "rebelle" qu'il fallait "saquer"....

> Rien ne pouvait m'intéresser davantage que ce "rebelle" qui avait voyagé dans pas mal d'établissements, subi d'incroyables tests de "réadaptation" avant d'émerger là: père et mère massacrés comme juifs durant la

guerre, enfance de fugitif, Georges Perec ne montrait alors qu'un besoin confus, encore mal expliqué, d'écrire.[3]

After receiving his *baccalauréat* in 1954, Perec spent six years (interrupted by his military service in 1958-59) writing, attending courses in history at the Sorbonne and supporting himself with occasional market studies and notes and articles which appeared in *La Nouvelle Nouvelle Revue Française* and *Les Lettres Nouvelles*. A trip to Yugoslavia during this period inspired a completed but never published novel, *L'Attentat de Saravejo,* loosely based on the 1914 assassination of the Archduke Ferdinand. Another completed novel, originally entitled *Gaspard pas mort,* was submitted as *Le Condottière* to Maurice Nadeau (*Les Lettres Nouvelles*) in 1959 shortly before his 1960 departure with Paulette, his wife of two days, for a year in Sfax, Tunisia.

The late fifties had been difficult years for Perec. Success as a writer was slow to come; he had little money and lived in the tiny apartment on the rue Saint-Honoré described in *Un Homme qui dort;* his psychological state, a sense of purposelessness approaching despair, closely paralleled that of the young protagonist of the novel.[4]

The Perecs' many Tunisian friends and the presence of Jean Duvignaud at the University of Tunis influenced their decision to escape their seemingly pointless life in Paris by going to Tunisia. Paulette obtained a teaching position at a *collège* in the provincial town of Sfax. During that year (1960-61), Georges wrote another unpublished novel, *J'avance masqué,* and also earned a *certificat de sociologie* through the University of Tunis.

Their life in Sfax was difficult. It was the time of the Algerian War and Arab-French relations were tense. Paulette's teaching position was frustrating. *Le Condottière* was refused by Nadeau. The scenes in *Les Choses* which narrate Jérôme and Sylvie's life in Sfax capture the emptiness and estrangement felt by the Perecs. They returned to Paris in 1961, a year earlier than originally expected, because of the growing political tension between France and Tunisia.

In 1961 Perec began work as a *documentaliste* at a neurophysiological laboratory of INSERM, a low-paying and unsatisfying position which he kept until 1978; despite his success as a writer during the late sixties and seventies, he was unable to support himself by his writing until the 1978 publication of *La Vie mode d'emploi*. He also published weekly crossword puzzles in *Le Point* and *Télérama,* which supplemented his income.

The 1965 publication of *Les Choses* by Nadeau's *Les Lettres Nouvelles* propelled Perec onto the French literary scene. Its notable success—Prix Renaudot, 100,000 copies sold, translations in sixteen languages—earned for Perec a significant literary reputation, which he maintained throughout the sixies and seventies and which reached a pinnacle when he received the *Prix Médicis* for *La Vie mode d'emploi.*

Late in the summer of 1981, Perec traveled to Australia to rest from a growing fatigue and to begin assembling materials for a new project, *53 Jours.* He returned to France in December and began writing, but at the time of his death from lung cancer on March 3, 1982, at the age of 45, he had finished only the first part of the novel.

• • •

The differences of style and subject in Perec's first three novels—*Les Choses* (1965), *Quel petit vélo* (1966), and *Un Homme qui dort* (1967) give the impression of a man with a need to write, searching for a personal means of expression. All three are based on life; *Quel petit vélo* was written to entertain; the other two represent an attempt to understand sociologically and psychologically two different periods in his life.

In 1967 Perec's friend Jacques Roubaud introduced him to the *Ouvroir de Littérature Potentielle* (Oulipo), a group of writers founded in 1960 by Raymond Queneau and François Le Lionnais. The group explored literary experimentation and especially constraint as a method of literary production. In 1969 Perec published his first novel directly inspired by his work with Oulipo, the remarkable *La Disparition,* 300 pages without the letter E. In the same year he begin assembling and organizing material for the masterpiece he would take ten years to complete, *La Vie mode d'emploi.*

The importance of literary experimentation in Perec's development as a writer is certain: through constraint he discovered imagination. But there is another, more significant factor in his development which surfaces in his autobiographical works of 1973-78: his discovery and gradual under-standing—with the aid of analysis—of the effect of his parents' death, especially his mother's, upon his creative imagination. His traumatic separation from her, her "disappearance," and his recognition, thirty years later, of the scars left upon his vision of the world, mark his works profoundly.

In his autobiographical novel, *W ou le souvenir d'enfance* (1975), Perec confronts his past, and the scars, and describes the persistence of disjointed imagery—images of suspension, closure, *coupure*—which constitutes an instinctive metaphorical reaction to his childhood trauma. Conscious of the disruption in his life which separates him from his past and from his heritage, Perec sifts the sands of time, looking for traces of his own passage. Proust without a madeleine, having only a fragmented, colorless impression of who he was, and unable to find consistent traces, Perec turns to writing to stem the erosion of his past:

> Ecrire, essayer méticuleusement de retenir quelque chose, de faire survivre quelque chose: arracher quelques bribes précises au vide qui se creuse, laisser, quelque part, un sillon, une trace, une marque ou quelques signes.[5]

In all of his works, from *Les Choses* to *La Vie mode d'emploi*, Perec creates characters bearing his curse who seek to create a present which is whole and meaningful and which carries their imprint. His various alter-egos will try to shape time and space to their will, will try to leave a permanent trace of their passage as a compensation for the broken strands of Perec's lost past.

1

THE EARLY NOVELS

Les Choses • *Quel petit vélo à guidon chromé au fond de la cour?* •
Un Homme qui dort

LES CHOSES, UNE HISTOIRE DES ANNEES SOIXANTE, PUBLISHED IN
1965,[1] was Perec's first novel, and his most successful until the 1978
publication of *La Vie mode d'emploi*. The novel was awarded the
prestigious Prix Renaudot and sold 100,000 copies, perhaps because, as
Jean Duvignaud notes,[2] a whole generation recognized itself in the portraits
of the novel's protagonists, Sylvie and Jérôme. At age twenty-nine, Perec
was clearly a rising star on the literary horizon.

The French press received the novel warmly and introduced the new
author to the world with appropriate praise. Robert Kanters set the tone:
"Le mérite de M. Perec est d'avoir nourri les cent pages de son roman d'une
analyse sociologique, et non psychologique, particulièrement perspicace.
La neutralité flaubertienne est constamment illuminée par l'intelligence la
plus aigüe."[3]   The reference to Flaubert is not gratuitous; as Kanters points
out, the boat "La Ville de Montereau," a picture of which adorns the wall of
Jérôme and Sylvie's ideal apartment, is the boat which in the opening scene
of *L'Education Sentimental* brings Frédéric Moreau to Paris. In an interview in the same issue of *Le Figaro*, Perec admits inserting thirty or forty
phrases from *L'Education Sentimentale* into his novel.[4]

Nor is the adjective "sociologique" accidental. Trained and employed as a sociologist, Perec himself stresses the sociological intent of his
novel in two published interviews.[5] While the story is the *Bildungsroman*
of Jérôme and Sylvie's "sentimental education," it is to be read, as the
subtitle informs us, as a generalized study of social behavior in a certain

milieu. Janick Arbois, overstating the author's intent, summarizes a possible reading of the novel: "L'auteur nous tient d'une main ferme le nez écrasé contre le bocal géant où il a enfermé ces deux spécimens humains qui ont 24 et 22 ans en 1960."[6]

Perec explains his design more gracefully: "Toute une sociologie américaine et française a commencé d'évoquer les problèmes de l'homme solitaire dans le monde de production.... Mais cela n'avait pas encore été un thème littéraire. Il n'y a pas encore eu de roman, de récit, qui présente des personnages vivant à l'intérieur de cette société, soumis à la pression du marché. C'est cela mon livre."[7] To study this phenomenon, Perec creates a young married couple who are trained as sociologists and employed as interviewers for market analyses. Their work exposes them to the products of a consumer society but doesn't pay them quite enough to permit them to enjoy all that they observe around them. The resulting frustration is the sociological message. Both Kanters and Arbois refer to Gabriel Marcel's distinction between *l'être* and *l'avoir,* suggesting that in their struggle to possess all the things that they desire, Jérôme and Sylvie sacrifice their identity. However, the question of the identity—or the individuality—of Jérôme and Sylvie, as stated in *Les Choses,* is more a conscious literary question than a sociological or existential one. They appear to lose their identity because of the process of abstraction, the generalization of their behavior, by which Perec relates his protagonists to their—and his—contemporaries.

Les Choses begins with a lengthy detailed description of an apartment. The narrator's "eye" (first word of the novel) guides us along the corridors, stopping to register the carpet and the walls, into and around each room, noting ornamental details and manifesting a geometric interest in the arrangement of the space.

We soon sense that this description in the conditional tense is neither a Balzacian generation of setting nor a Robbe-Grilletian display of objective reality.[8] The description is humanized, brought to life, by phrases which idealize the setting: "un peu triste" (12), "elle serait havre de paix, terre de bonheur" (13), "La vie, là, serait facile, serait simple" (15), "Il serait agréable de venir s'y asseoir" (15), "Ils appelleraient cet équilibre bonheur" (16).

The brusque changes of tense which follow the introductory description—first a paragraph in the conditional perfect, and then the dominant imperfect—suggest a vision isolated from the narrative. Later in the novel, when we follow Jérôme and Sylvie into the world of market samples, advertising, and the temptations of material comforts, we understand that the passage is a collective dream, of Jérôme and Sylvie but also of their generalized (by the pronoun *ils*) friends, whose desires become fixed upon the trappings of material ornamentation, which the novel summarizes as, "ces choses belles et simples, douces, lumineuses" (16). These "things," these desirable objects which agreeably fill living space are a goal for the protagonists and the subject matter of *Les Choses*.

The passage's geometric meticulousness and the insistence on the interrelationship of desired objects raise the nature of the characters' obsession from a simple desire for objects to a more complex dream of organized space. As has been pointed out, the description reads like an advertising prospectus[9] or a *Better Homes and Gardens* article. It represents the vision of an interior decorator who blends, harmonizes, juxtaposes and contrasts elements of decoration designed to create ideal living space.

The characters' spatial consciousness begins with their awareness of differences in types of space:

> Il leur fallut longtemps pour s'apercevoir que les fonctions les plus banales de la vie de tous les jours—dormir, manger, lire, bavarder, se laver—exigeaient chacune un espace spécifique, dont l'absence notoire commença dès lors à se faire sentir. (19)

Their growing consciousness creates new needs. The lack of appropriate spaces becomes for Jérôme and Sylvie a "tyrannical" problem.

Their ideal apartment possesses of course spaces appropriate for all of their activities, spaces which their imagination fills with lists of things, catalogs of desirable objects which fit together and form a harmonious vision. Thus the three knickknack shelves contain, "des agates, et des œufs de pierre, des boîtes à priser, des bonbonnières, des cendriers de jade, une coquille de nacre, une montre de gousset en argent, un verre taillé, une pyramide de cristal, une miniature dans un cadre ovale" (12).

The grouping of desirable items to fill a space agreeably is extended to far larger spaces: a farm or a city. The cataloging of Parisian space takes the form of desirable itineraries: "Ils laissaient derrière eux le Treizième tout proche, dont ils ne connaissaient guère que l'avenue des Gobelins, à cause de ses quatre cinémas, évitant la sinistre rue Cuvier, qui ne les eût conduits qu'aux abords plus sinistres encore de la gare d'Austerlitz, et empruntaient, presque invariablement, la rue Monge, puis la rue des Ecoles, gagnaient Saint-Michel, Saint-Germain, et, de là, selon les jours où les saisons, le Palais-Royal, l'Opéra, ou la gare Montparnasse, Vavin, la rue d'Assas, Saint-Sulpice, le Luxembourg" (78-79).

The planning of an itinerary becomes a form of exterior decorating, a planning of large spatial areas to create harmonies and exclude sinister areas. Just as in the decoration of their ideal apartment they are limited by the range of possible materials, colors and shapes, in their planning of an ideal itinerary, they are limited by the geography of Paris upon which they attempt to impose their specific tastes.

Their arrangement of an ideal universe knows no such limits. Inspired by a visit to a farm to which their work had led them, Jérôme and Sylvie build upon the catalog of real rustic delights—granaries full of wheat, rows of shiny tractors, old venerable pieces of furniture, barrels and jars full of wine and oil and honey, smoked hams, crates of apples and pears—a "mirage" of immense marketplaces, offering an abundance of wonderful things to eat, organized and cataloged through two pages (89-90). Closing their eyes, Sylvie and Jérôme look beyond these fabulous markets and fill the imaginary space with tall cities made of steel, wood, glass, and marble, with swimming pools (in the sky!), patios, theaters, gardens, aquariums, jungles, oceans, mazes—all designed for their pleasure, "un paysage achevé, une totalité spectaculaire et triomphale, une complète image du monde, une organization cohérente qu'ils pouvaient enfin comprendre, déchiffrer" (93).

The vivid evocation of their fabulous dreams intensifies their sensations and brings them to new levels of consciousness:

> Il leur semblait d'abord que leurs sensations se décuplaient, que s'amplifiaient à l'infini leurs facultés de voir et sentir, qu'un bonheur merveilleux accompagnait le moindre de leurs gestes, rythmait leurs pas, imprégnait leur vie: le monde allait à eux, ils allaient au-devant du monde, ils n'en finissaient pas de le découvrir. Leur vie était amour et ivresse. Leur passion ne connaissait pas de limites, leur liberté était sans contrainte. (93)

Their imagination carries them far from their earlier dream of a tranquil "havre de paix, terre de bonheur." Their desire to fill space with meaningful, coherent structures inspires this grandiose image of a mythical, harmonious garden of urban beauty and pleasure. Jérôme and Sylvie, creators of this organized universe, conquerors of space, architects of perfection, experience an intoxicating surge of power, the certainty of freedom, the rapture of omnipotence.

The novel's two dreams of ideal space dissipate quickly and dramatically, overwhelmed by the reality of Sylvie and Jérôme's quotidian surroundings. A change of tense marks the descent from the hypothetical (conditional) description of the ideal apartment. A paragraph in the conditional perfect negates it: "Ils auraient aimé être riches.... Leurs plaisirs auraient été intenses.... Ils auraient aimé vivre.... Leur vie aurait été un art de vivre." (17) The next paragraph in the imperfect establishes their reality: "Pour ce jeune couple, qui n'était pas riche, mais que désirait l'être... il n'existait pas de situation plus inconfortable.... Ils étaient renvoyés, alors que déjà ils rêvaient d'espaces, de lumière, de silence, à la réalité, même pas sinistre, mais simplement rétrécie... de leur logement exigu, de leurs repas quotidiens, de leurs vacances chétives.... C'était leur réalité, ils n'en avaient pas d'autre."

The more grandiose dream of a universe organized according to their desires disintegrates because of the intrusion of reality, but the nature of the dream itself makes its disintegration more complete and more crushing:

> Mais ils étouffaient sous l'amoncellement des détails. Les images s'estompaient, se brouillaient; ils n'en pouvaient retenir que quelques bribes, floues et confuses, fragiles, obsédantes et bêtes, appauvries. Non plus un mouvement d'ensemble, mais des tableaux isolés, non plus une unité sereine, mais une fragmentation crispée, comme si ces images n'avaient jamais été que des reflets très lointains, démesurément obscurcis, des scintillations allusives, illusoires, qui s'évanouissent à peine nées, des poussières: la dérisoire projection de leurs désirs les plus gauches, un impalpable poudroiement de maigres splendeurs, des lambeaux de rêves qu'ils ne pouvaient jamais saisir.

Their dream of a planned universe, filled with visions of harmony and wholeness, splits into isolated particles, each of which reflects only a single derisive element of their coordinated yearning. The fragmented dream, weighted as it is with so many things, becomes destructive, suffocating. Two paragraphs later the first part of the novel ends with the sentence, "Ils se sentaient écrasés." Their exploded vision leaves Jérôme and Sylvie with the awful knowledge that their dreams as well as their lives are unlivable.

Perec subtitles his novel, "Une histoire des années soixante," in order to emphasize that the dreams and frustrations of Jérôme and Sylvie were shared by a whole generation. Several stylistic elements reinforce this generalization. The first few pages of the novel describe the ideal apartment without at all personalizing the vision ("L'œil, d'abord, glisserait sur la moquette..."). The initial subjective reactions are associated with an anonymous subject: "La vie, là, serait facile, serait simple." When finally a personal pronoun is introduced, it is a very vague "ils," introduced on page 15, and whose antecedent is not revealed until page 20. Finally on page 26 we learn who "ils" are, but are told little about them. Sylvie and Jérôme's existence as a "cellular"[10] couple, two partners who throughout the first part of the novel and a good deal of the second are indistinguishable, one from the other, also tends to generalize their experience. The "ils" which at first describes them becomes further extended as the novel progresses, for Sylvie and Jérôme are associated, merged, with their friends who belong to the same milieu (advertising) and have the same tastes, dreams, and frustrations. The narration goes to great lengths to group together a large segment of the population using the pronoun "ils":

> Ils étaient donc de leur temps. Ils étaient bien dans leur peau. Ils n'étaient pas, disaient-ils, tout à fait dupes. Ils savaient garder leurs distances. Ils étaient décontractés, ou du moins tentaient de l'être. Ils avaient de l'humour. Ils étaient loin d'être bêtes. (44)

> Leurs appartements, studios, greniers, deux pièces de maisons vétustes, dans des quartiers choisis—le Palais-Royal, la contrescarpe, Saint-Germain, le Luxembourg, Montparnasse—se ressemblaient: on y retrouvait les mêmes canapés crasseux, les mêmes tables dites rustiques, les mêmes amoncellements de livres et de disques, les mêmes vieux pots, vieilles bouteilles, vieux verres, vieux bocaux, indifféremment remplis de fleurs, de crayons, de menue monnaie, de cigarettes, de bonbons, de trombones. Ils étaient vêtus, en gros, de la même façon...
> (38)

The uniformity of their tastes helps to cement friendships by creating a reassuring unity of surroundings from one apartment to another. This cohesiveness, which flatters their vanity and self-esteem, extends not only to their decorations and clothing, but also to their opinions, what they eat and drink, what movies they watch, which cafés they frequent.

Perec finds an apt symbol to characterize the life-style, decorations, clothing, and opinions of the group: *L'Express*. "*L'Express* et lui seul, correspondait à leur art de vivre; ils retrouvaient en lui... les préoccupations les plus courantes de leur vie de tous les jours" (38-39).

Sylvie and Jérôme, though inextricably associated with this generation whose every activity and thought is reflected in the pages of *L'Express,* distinguish themselves from the others in one important way: they suffer more. All of the members of their group are victims of the world which they are creating, the world of advertising and marketing which predicates a life-style based on the principle: "désirer toujours plus qu'on ne [peut] acquérir" (43). In order to live the life they desire, Sylvie and Jérôme need to acquire wealth, but they scorn this first important step. In their impatience to satisfy their desires, they refuse to accept a life of slow accumulation: they don't want to arrive, they want to have arrived. And so they dream of ways of acquiring a fortune rapidly: inheritance, lottery, gambling, a found purse, pearls in an oyster shell, priceless antiques bought for a trifle, even theft. But they do nothing in the real world and doom themselves to discontentment:

> Les gens qui choisissent de gagner d'abord de l'argent, ceux qui réservent pour plus tard, pour quand ils seront riches, leurs vrais projets, n'ont pas forcément tort. Ceux qui ne veulent que vivre, et qui appellent vie la liberté la plus grande, la seule poursuite du bonheur, l'exclusif assouvissement de leurs désirs, ou de leurs instincts, l'usage immédiat des richesses illimitées du monde—Jérôme et Sylvie avaient fait leur ce vaste programme—, ceux-là seront toujours malheureux. (58)

They refuse to sacrifice their freedom for advancement. As the years pass, Sylvie and Jérôme distinguish themselves increasingly from the pack by their refusal to devote themselves to their careers and the pursuit of wealth. To preserve their freedom, Sylvie and Jérôme accept only occasional field assignment work, interviews, and surveys. They both try a few weeks of more lucrative office assignments, but find regular hours, rush hour subways, and getting up early distastefully confining. They find themselves caught, crushed, between their desire for freedom and flexibility on one hand and on the other, their fears of economic distress:

> Mais des dangers les guettaient de toutes parts. Ils auraient voulu que
> leur histoire soit l'histoire du bonheur; elle n'était, trop souvent, que
> celle d'un bonheur menacé. Ils étaient encore jeunes, mais le temps
> passait vite.... Ils avaient peur. (62)

A new danger threatens the precarious course they have chosen
between freedom and security: time, whose passage for the still young (not
yet thirty) couple becomes an obsessive preoccupation. Time passes
unevenly through their lives. The first four years of their professional work
were spent in discovery of "life" as it is revealed to them through their
market surveys. The years are summarized by two pages of questions:
"Pourquoi les aspirateurs-traîneaux se vendent-ils si mal?" "Aime-t-on la
purée toute faite?" "Que pense-t-on, dans le milieu de modeste extraction,
de la chicorée?" "A quoi fait-on d'abord attention en mangeant un yaourt?"
"Quelles qualités demandez-vous à votre matelas?" Perec catalogs the
subjects of their inquiries and concludes ironically, "Rien de ce qui était
humain ne leur fut étranger" (30). These four years of "questioning" lead to
the discovery of "things," the desirable objects of life, which eventually
occupy their thoughts and activities.

The Algerian War aroused sufficient emotion in Sylvie and Jérôme
that they joined an Anti-Fascist Committee and participated in a few
demonstrations—not sure why they were there and what they were doing in
such "sinister" areas as La Place de la Bastille, La Place de la Nation, and
La Place de l'Hôtel de Ville. The end of the war brings an end to their
political consciousness and marks a new period in their lives. They look
back, conscious that time has passed:

> Sept années d'un seul coup basculaient dans le passé: leurs années
> d'étudiants, les années de leurs rencontres, les meilleures années de leur
> vie.

> Peut-être rien n'avait-il changé. Il leur arrivait encore de se mettre à
> leurs fenêtres, de regarder la cour, les petits jardins, le maronnier,
> d'écouter chanter les oiseaux. D'autres livres, d'autres disques étaient
> venus s'empiler sur les étagères branlantes. Le diamant de l'électro-
> phone commençait à être usé. (73)

Sensitive to changes in their material surroundings, trivial though they may
be, Sylvie and Jérôme find everywhere symbols of the passage of time.

The wearing out of the phonograph needle corresponds to an analogous wearing out of their lives: invisible on a day-to-day basis, but evident when seen in the perspective of seven years.

The disintegration of their individual lives becomes generalized. The group too begins to break apart: that harmonious wholeness, summarized by the pronoun *ils* and chronicled weekly in the pages of *L'Express* begins to unravel in time:

> Mais les amitiés aussi s'effilochaient. Certains soirs, dans le champ clos de leurs pièces exigües, les couples réunis s'affrontaient du regard et de la voix. Certains soirs, ils comprenaient enfin que leur si belle amitié, leur vocabulaire presque initiatique, leurs gags intimes, ce monde commun, ces gestes communs qu'ils avaient forgés, ne renvoyaient à rien: c'était un univers ratatiné, un monde à bout de souffle qui ne débouchait sur rien. Leur vie n'était pas conquête, elle était effritement, dispersion. (76)

Anguished by these early premonitions of the ravages of time and crushed by the disintegration of their lives, by the sundering of their friendships, by the breaking apart of all of their visions of harmony and wholeness, Sylvie and Jérôme find themselves desperately alone and empty. Unable to go back, to put back together what has in the course of time come apart, unable to change their course or the course of time, they attempt to flee, to flee from their shattered illusions, their lives, their dreams, their friends, and from the "things" which had been the dominant symbols of the harmony of their lives and dreams.

The second part of the novel is as different from the first as Sfax, Tunisia, is from Paris. In a novelistic universe obsessed with space, the transfer of the action from one place to another is dramatic. Fleeing from all that surrounded and constituted their lives, Sylvie and Jérôme also in a sense flee from themselves. They become new people with new occupations and new concerns. They exchange a universe too charged with things, too full, for a universe which is, from their point of view, too empty.

Before their real departure, there is a series of false departures: dreams of other lives, of simpler lives. Their real departure is somewhat accidental. Almost mechanically they respond to a newspaper announcement for teachers in Tunisia. Almost without knowing why, they find themselves in the provincial town of Sfax, with Sylvie employed as a teacher and Jérôme unemployed. Their Tunisian apartment overwhelms them:

> C'était une demeure triste et froide. Les murs trop hauts, recouverts d'une sorte de chaux ocre jaune qui s'en allait par grandes plaques, les sols uniformément dallés de grands carreaux sans couleur, l'espace inutile, tout était trop grand, trop nu, pour qu'ils puissent l'habiter. Il aurait fallu qu'ils soient cinq ou six, quelques bons amis, en train de boire, de manger, de parler. Mais ils étaient seuls, perdus. (103)

Accustomed to a cramped apartment, crowded with things and people, they feel lost in the emptiness of their new surroundings. An even more oppressive sensation of alienation overcomes them when they venture out into the surrounding space of Sfax:

> Cette sensation d'étrangeté s'accentuait, devenait presque oppressante, lorsque, ayant devant eux des longs après-midi vides, des dimanches désespérants, ils traversaient la ville arabe de part en part, et, au-delà de Bab Djabi, gagnaient les interminables faubourgs de Sfax. Sur des kilomètres, c'étaient des jardins minuscules, des haies de figuiers de Barbarie, des maisons de torchis, des cabanes de tôle et de carton; puis d'immenses lagunes désertes et putrides, et, tout au bout, à l'infini, les premiers champs d'oliviers; ils passaient devant des casernes, traversaient des terrains vagues, des zones bourbeuses. (106)

The picturesque *couleur locale* of North Africa is transformed by the vision of Sylvie and Jérôme for whom afternoons are long and empty, suburbs are interminable, lagoons putrid and deserted, and for whom the perspective of infinite rows of olive trees is dispiriting. Their perception is selective; they observe only those details of the countryside which are empty, made of cardboard and sheet metal, and completely colorless.

Surrounded by space whose emptiness crushes them even more than the crowded space and dreams of their Parisian life, Sylvie and Jérôme begin to feel that they are excluded from a world whose reality they doubt:

> Nulle âme qui vive: derrière les portes toujours closes, rien d'autre que des corridors nus, des escaliers de pierre, des cours aveugles. Des suites de rues se coupant à angle droit, des rideaux de fer, des palissades, un monde de fausses rues, d'avenues fantômes. Ils marchaient, silencieux,

désorientés, et ils avaient parfois l'impression que tout n'était qu'illusion, que Sfax n'existait pas, ne respirait pas. (110)

Sylvie and Jérôme find in the walls, closed doors, and courtyards of Sfax symbols of their exclusion. They are cut off, isolated, to the extent that they are disoriented and partially blinded. They cannot see or imagine the reality of Sfax; their troubled vision cannot penetrate the geometric outline of the city.

They take trips outside of Sfax, trying to escape the apparent emptiness of their surroundings, trying to find an identifiable, familiar space, "Mais, le plus souvent, ils ne quittaient Sfax que pour retrouver, quelques dizaines ou quelques centaines de kilomètres plus loin, les mêmes rues mornes, les mêmes souks grouillants et incompréhensibles, les mêmes lagunes, les mêmes palmiers lourds, la même aridité" (144). The country-side appears to them as an empty "croûte blanchâtre" (115), littered here and there with empty, hollow objects, "une carcasse d'âne, un vieux bidon rouillé, un entassement de pierres à demi éboulé qui avait peut-être été une maison" (115).

The description of their travels, summarized by catalogs of empty names, juxtaposes the general with the specific; several paragraphs in the imperfect tense present landscapes and urban scenes which to others might have appeared lively, quaint, even fascinating, but which flow together in an uncertain and unreal chronology, reflecting the morbid indifference of Sylvie and Jérôme, "Et ils ne rapportaient de ces voyages que des images de vide, de sécheresse..." (117).

This empty vision which accompanies their travels throughout Tunisia fails to distinguish space and time. Scenes melt together, as do moments. Time which might have appeared to them as a savior—they are obligated to spend only eight months in Sfax—becomes as empty and meaningless as their surroundings:

> Il put sembler bientôt que toute vie s'arrêtait en eux. Du temps passait, immobile. Plus rien ne les reliait au monde, sinon des journaux toujours trop vieux dont ils n'étaient même pas sûrs qu'ils ne fussent pas que de pieux mensonges, les souvenirs d'une vie antérieure, les reflets d'un autre monde. Ils avaient toujours vécu à Sfax et ils y vivraient toujours. Ils n'avaient plus de projets, plus d'impatience; ils n'attendaient rien, pas même des vacances toujours trop lointaines, pas même un retour en France. (111-12)

Their perception becomes increasingly somnambulistic. Rejected by space and time, they forget their past dreams, forget their past, as they float through an eternal, disorienting present. The main body of the novel ends with basic but unanswered questions: "Et puis? Qu'avaient-ils fait? Que s'était-il passé?" (120).

The Epilogue hypothesizes their future life in Tunisia presenting the most likely eventuality of their return to France and their acceptance of secure but unglamorous positions in Bordeaux. Perec steps back from his characters, abandoning them, "sur la pointe des pieds,"[11] attempting a graceful exit. A happy ending, that is, a satisfying life for Jérôme and Sylvie in the advertising milieu of Bordeaux, is impossible. To continue to follow them through the disappointments and frustrations of provincial life would be unnecessarily cruel. Instead, Perec suggests what awaits them in the often quoted last sentence of the novel which refers to their experience in the dining car of the SNCF train carrying them to Bordeaux: "Mais le repas qu'on leur servira sera franchement insipide" (130).

For Jérôme and Sylvie, who first fail to find spaces which conform to their desires and who ultimately find themselves locked in a continuous present with no desires to fill their space, there is no Proustian redemption of lost time found, no valorisation of experiences, illusions, and disappointments. Time advances and space surrounds them, indifferent to their yearnings.

Their "sentimental education" leaves them with no illusions, but also with no dreams, or even plans. They have grown older, but the only effect of time's passage seems to be decay, first of their dreams and friendships, and eventually of their will. Conscious of the grinding away of their lives, of fragmentation, of dispersion, they attempt to flee the surroundings which have failed to respond to their desire for wholeness and harmony, and find themselves in another world which may be whole, but is empty.

Life seems to force its insipid meals upon Jérôme and Sylvie, not as a result of any notorious defects in their characters, but because of the nature of space and time whose promises are not kept and which work together to cancel dreams, frustrate expectations, and wear away the human fiber. *Les Choses* is the story of Jérôme and Sylvie's failure to respond creatively to the time and space which are theirs.

• • •

Within just a few months of the publication and triumph of *Les Choses,* Perec published his second novel, *Quel petit vélo à guidon chromé au fond de la cour?*[12] Based on a real experience of Perec's 1958-59 military service, *Quel petit vélo* is dedicated to "L. G. en mémoire de son plus beau fait d'armes." L. G. are the initials of *Ligne Générale,* a group of radical critics opposed to the Algerian War with whom Perec collaborated on articles which were published in *Partisans* in 1962 and 1963.[13]

The novel's title "à la façon d'une comédie musicale,"[14] and tongue-in-cheek title page description suggest the tone of the narrative: "Récit épique en prose agrémenté d'ornements versifiés tirés des meilleurs auteurs—par l'auteur de *Comment rendre service à ses amis* (ouvrage couronné par diverses Académies Militaires)." Using parodied quotes, popular idiomatic language patterns, mock epic style, and indexed rhetorical devices[15]—alliteration, anacoluthon, apostrophe, hyperbole, litotes, metonymy, prosopopoeia, onomatopoeia, etc.—the book tells a simple comic tale about the efforts of some well-meaning friends to keep a young soldier[16] from being sent to fight in the Algerian War. Most of the action takes place one night when the twelve friends have a meal for the soldier and put their plan into action: a faked suicide attempt designed to land him in a psychiatric hospital. The plan fails only because the hero vomits up the barbituates he had taken, along with three-fourths of a bottle of gin and the rest of the epic feast.

The pills were purchased at a pharmacy located at the corner of the rue Boris Vian and the rue Teilhard de Chardin. Several allusions to this apparently central intersection suggest that the literary plane of the novel exists at the point where wit and imagination encounter phenomenological speculation; the heroes of the novel sit in cafés discussing, "Lukasse, Heliphore, Hégueule et autres olibrii de la même farine" (18). The influence of Vian is clearly perceptible in several puns: "La jambe moulée dans une paire de djinns" (18), "Dans tous les bourreaux de poste" (31), "A brûle-tourcoing nous lui demandâmes..." (61). Other sources for the novel's humor are Alphonse Allais, Alfred Jarry, Céline, Henri Michaux, and Raymond Queneau.

Perec's friend Harry Mathews characterizes the novel as "une œuvre mineure" and speaks of two stylistic concerns which guided its composition: "l'épuisement systématique d'une somme de formes rhétoriques," and "la répétition de mots ou même de phrases formant à travers tout le livre une trame enjouée."[17] The rhetorical forms, mostly parodied, are epic devices and other figures which are indexed along with some self-indulgent entries ("Métaphore incohérente," "Nécrologie, ben voyons," "Helvétisme, y'en a pas," "Hispanisme, y'en a pas non plus"). Mathews associates Perec's interest in rhetorical devices with a course given by Roland Barthes and a recent reading of *Ulysses*.

Some of the novel's more interesting figures include:

> Et Apollon, majestueux, n'en finissait pas d'arriver au Zénith. Les heures s'écoulaient comme au travers d'un sablier empli de grès (le lecteur déplorera sans doute la platitude de cette image: qu'il en apprécie, pourtant, la pertinence géologique.) (14-15)

> Alors les bureaucrates, les sales planqués du service des Effectifs, ouvrirent leurs grands registres reliés de toile flammée et pointèrent de leurs grands doigts maigres de Parques parkinsonniennes les noms de tous les ceusses qui s'en iraient bientôt faire les zouaves. (39)

> Enfin, sur le coup de neuf heures moins le quart, alors que le désespoir aux doigts crochus et aux dents déchaussées commençaient à envahir la place... (59)

> Et le lendemain, à peine la douce aurore aux doigts boudinés eût-elle tiré du lit, non sans difficulté, le gars Phoebus... (29)

Examples of words and phrases repeated throughout the novel include the references to the motorcycle of the novel's title, the variations on the name of the soldier, and the many references to the birthplace of Henri Pollak:

> son Montparnasse natal (car il était né à Montparnasse) (14)
> natif de Montparnasse où qu'il avait venu au monde (21)
> son natal Montparnasse (car c'est là qu'il avait né) (15)
> son Montparnasse qui lui avait donné le jour (17)
> son natal Montparnasse qui l'avait vu naître (23)

Perec wrote and published *Quel petit vélo* to amuse himself, his friends, and the public. Robert Kanters's judgment of the novel's literary interest does not appear unduly severe:[18]

Tout cela vaut par la manière, c'est-à-dire par la verve gouailleuse, et M. Perec n'en manque pas. Il invente mille drôleries dans le style homérique et dans le goût à la mode, il les répète, les varie avec plus ou moins de bonheur... il a le sens du bouffon et il y réussit très bien. Ce que l'on pourrait dire peut-être, c'est que la bouffonnerie par nature ne peut pas durer très longtemps: mais le livre est très court. Et aussi qu'il y a dans cette ironie savante, dans cette parodie appuyée, dans cet humour aux formes élaborées quelque chose d'un peu scolaire, pour ne pas dire d'un peu cuistre.

In an interview with Jean Duvignaud[19] Perec discusses his work in progress, *Un Homme qui dort,*[20] and compares it with the recently published *Les Choses:*

Par une sorte de reflexe instantané, après avoir fini ce livre, où j'ai essayé de décrire la fascination des choses, la pression qu'elles exercent, je suis revenu en arrière dans ma vie personnelle. J'écris un livre sur une période de ma vie où, au contraire, j'étais absolument indifférent. Ce n'est plus la fascination, mais le "refus" des choses, le refus du monde. De même que le premier s'appelait "Les Choses," celui-là pourrait s'appeler "les autres." Ce n'est pas du tout l'impossibilité de communiquer; ce n'est pas du tout métaphysique. C'est vraiment l'histoire de quelqu'un qui, un jour, a envie de dire, "Foutez-moi la paix! Laissez-moi tranquille," qui ne passe pas un examen, et qui traîne pendant deux ans.

Dans "Les Choses," je décris Paris comme une ville assez fascinante, assez belle. Et là, maintenant, je voudrais décrire une sorte de Paris absolument impossible, très noir, c'est-à-dire le vide, le contraire de la chaleur.

Three elements dominate the author's perception of his work in progress: his own personal identification with the protagonist, the lack of a metaphysical dimension, and the emptiness of the world he is describing.

In the interview Perec doesn't mention the novel's form, the use of the second person familiar pronoun and the relationship which this establishes between narrator and protagonist. Both Marc Slonim[21] and John Gilbert[22] point to the influence of Michel Butor; Gilbert also mentions Monique Wittig's *L'Opoponax* as a possible source, for it, like Perec's "tu," creates "the identification with Everyman, the reader."

Camus's Jean-Baptiste Clamence uses "vous" in his narrative to include the reader in a similar fashion.

Etienne Lalou[23] and Bernard Pingaud[24] comment in very similar terms on the distinction created between narrator and protagonist by the form of the narration. Pingaud associates the form with Kafka:

> Ce "tu" auquel s'adresse le narrateur c'est évidemment lui-même. Mais un lui-même décalé, un lui-même autre... le tu qu'emploie Kafka dans certains fragments (l'un d'eux figure en épigraphe du livre) pour figurer devant lui quelqu'un où il se reconnaît, sans pourtant se confondre avec lui: Homme "neutre," insaisissable, mais complice, à la fois accusé et victime, que l'œuvre... ne cessera plus de questionner.

Lalou emphasizes the detachment which the "tu" creates with respect to the protagonist: "Le héros n'a ni nom ni prénom. Il n'est pas le narrateur (il dirait "je") ni le raconté (l'auteur dirait "il"). Il est le tutoyé, celui auquel on s'adresse d'un ton un peu protecteur, un peu humoristique, mais où perce la complicité. Il est le copain, le frère, l'autre soi-même." Lalou might have added, the younger brother, whom the narrator places at a distance from himself to judge and ultimately to condemn.

• • •

Un Homme qui dort analyzes in minute detail the progression of an individual's intellectual adventure through a series of interrelated states to an ambiguous conclusion. The protagonist is a twenty-five-year-old sociology student who one day experiences a moral crisis which alters his attitude and conduct:

> Il a suffi, il a presque suff, un jour de mai où il faisait trop chaud, de l'inopportune conjonction d'un texte dont tu avais perdu le fil, d'un bol de Nescafé au goût soudain trop amer, et d'une bassine de matière plastique rose remplie d'une eau noirâtre où flottait six chaussettes, pour que quelque chose se casse, s'altère, se défasse, et qu'apparaisse au grand jour—mais le jour n'est jamais grand dans la chambre de bonne de la rue Saint-Honoré—cette vérité décevante, triste et ridicule comme un bonnet d'âne, lourde comme un dictionnaire Gaffiot: tu n'as pas envie de poursuivre, ni de te défendre, ni d'attaquer. (29)

Fatigue, nonchalance, and lassitude overcome the student in one moment's sudden illumination: desire, ambition, pride, and determination all disappear in the wake of a transformation brought on, to a great extent, by a series of concurrent perceptions—the bitter taste of his coffee, the lost thread of the text he was reading, and the sight of a basin full of soaking socks.[25] Through these physical sensations is born an overwhelming and inexplicable negative impulse not to go on. Here begins the first brief phase of the protagonist's adventure: an involuntary passivity which will soon give way to a longer and more controlled phase: a studied indifference, the attempt to repress systematically intellectual and emotional reactions.

The passive phase of the adventure is characterized by words such as "lourdeur," "lassitude," "tièdeur," "torpeur," "bourdonnement," and "somnambule." The somnambulistic young man spends the summer months at his parents' home near Auxerre. A series of paragraphs with dominant action verb topic sentences summarizes his life there:

> Tu restes là plusieurs mois...
> Tu parles à peine à tes parents...
> Tu t'assieds à la table...
> Tu descends au village...
> Tu longes les maisons restaurées...
> Tu pars en promenade... (41-43)

All of these acts without volition, this drifting without purpose, this stagnation, brings him into contact with nature: "La nature est là qui t'invite et qui t'aime" (44). Neither inspired nor moved by the beauties of nature, he finds himself nonetheless fascinated by certain phenomena; his fascination with a tree leads him to the next phase of his adventure. The tree's indifference to him, which he contrasts with the joyful playfulness of a dog, inspires his admiration: "Tu ne peux rester neutre en face d'un chien, pas plus qu'en face d'un homme. Mais tu ne dialogueras jamais avec un arbre... l'arbre ne te demande rien... tu ne seras jamais maître de l'arbre. Tu ne pourras jamais que vouloir devenir arbre à ton tour" (46).

During his last days in the country he begins to realize this project which he will explore more methodically upon his return to Paris: to become a tree. In the Jardin du Luxembourg, he finds a human model:

> Sur un banc non loin de toi, un vieillard momifié, immobile, les pieds
> joints, le menton appuyé sur le pommeau de sa canne qu'il agrippe à

> deux mains, regarde devant lui dans le vide, pendant des heures. Tu l'admires. Tu cherches son secret, sa faiblesse. Mais il semble inattaquable. Il doit être sourd comme un pot, à moitié aveugle et plutôt paralytique. Mais il ne bave même pas, il ne remue pas les lèvres, il cille à peine. Le soleil tourne autour de lui.... Il ressemble à une statue, mais il a sur les statues l'avantage de pouvoir se lever et marcher, s'il le désire. Il ressemble aussi à un être humain... mais il a sur les autres êtres humains ce privilège de pouvoir rester immobile comme une statue, pendant des heures et des heures, sans efforts apparents. Tu voudrais y parvenir, mais, sans doute est-ce l'un des effets de ton extrême jeunesse dans la vocation de vieillard, tu t'énerves trop vite: malgré toi, ton pied remue sur le sable, tes yeux errent, tes doigts croisent et décroisent sans cesse. (69-70)

The old man resembles a statue about whom the sun turns! This human statue represents a state of indifference, a mastery of life, comparable to that of the tree, and a much more likely model for a young man in pursuit of indifference. At first incapable of perfect imitation of the old man, the student invents exercises, disciplined tasks, designed to educate his indifference: he reads *Le Monde,* line by line, paying attention to every word, even noting the circulation and name of the press where it was printed. But he trains himself to remember nothing and to show no interest in any of the events reported.

During his daily walks around Paris, the indifferent hero forces upon himself tasks such as compiling catalogs: "Tu dénombres les églises, les statues équestres, les pissotières, les restaurants russes" (79). He plays solitaire, follows the lines of cracks in the ceiling of his room, goes to galleries to study indifferently the exposed works, and thumbs indifferently books in a bookstore. In his choice of foods to eat he concentrates only on providing nourishment: "Nul point d'exclamation n'accompagne tes repas. Tu manges de la viande et des frites, tu bois du vin" (76).

In time the student's efforts are successful:

> Avec le temps, ta froideur devient fabuleuse. Tes yeux ont perdu tout ce qui faisait leur éclat, ta silhouette s'est faite parfaitement tombante. Une sérénité sans lassitude, sans amertume, s'inscrit au coin de tes lèvres. Tu glisses dans les rues, intouchable, protégé par l'usure pondérée de tes vêtements, par la neutralité de tes pas. (97)

"Froideur," "sérénité," "intouchable," "protégé," "neutralité": he seems to have achieved his goal, to have attained the status of a tree/statue. He wanders through the city, immune to its emotions, demands, and desires. His reflexes are dulled to the most elementary level. He is a robot, an eye, a camera which records mechanically, a rat abandoned to its memorized labyrinth. But his triumph is far from complete, for his inviolability proves to be an ephemeral illusion:

> Libre comme une vache, comme une huître, comme un rat! Mais les rats ne cherchent pas le sommeil pendant des heures. Mais les rats ne se réveillent pas en sursaut, pris de panique, trempés de sueur...
> Mais les rats ne se rongent pas les ongles, et surtout pas méthodiquement, pendant des heures entières, jusqu'à ce que l'extrémité de leurs griffes ne sont plus qu'une plaie diffuse. (119-20)

The operation was successful, but the patient is filled with anguish. Indifferent by day, he is tormented at night by dreams of torture. Gradually this nighttime anguish imposes itself upon his daytime peregrinations and drags him into the next phase of his adventure:

> Le malheur n'a pas fondu sur toi, ne s'est pas abattu sur toi; il s'est infiltré avec lenteur, il s'est insinué presque suavement. Il a minutieusement imprégné ta vie, tes gestes, tes heures, ta chambre, comme une vérité longtemps masquée, comme une évidence refusée. (124)

Slowly but certainly comes the revelation that the search for inviolability behind the mask of indifference is a trap, and that all he has achieved is an alienated solitude which still leaves him prey to all of the terrors of the human condition. The condition of laboratory rat has turned against him, and the hideous, terrifying monsters of life confront him, as his new brethren:

> Bannis, parias, exclus, porteurs d'invisibles étoiles... les somnambules, les brutes, les vieillards, les idiots, les sourds-muets... les ivrognes, les gâteux... les veuves, les sournois, les ancêtres, les fouineurs. (129)

The novel's most poetic pages evoke in these terms the hideous crowd who recognize in the protagonist one of their own and try to claim him.

The ambiguous conclusion of the adventure condemns the experience of indifference without suggesting a new life stance which can save the protagonist from his terror and his solitude: "Tu n'as rien appris, sinon que la solitude n'apprend rien, que l'indifférence n'apprend rien; c'était un leurre, une illusion fascinante et piégée" (158). He repeats three times that he has not died, not gone crazy; and yet the last sentence of the novel leaves him alone and afraid: "Tu as peur, tu attends. Tu attends, place Clichy, que la pluie cesse de tomber" (163).

• • •

The student's psychological adventure is also a literary pilgrimage with stops at several sacred shrines. The novel's title is an allusion to Proust.[26] The epigraph is a quote from Kafka which relates thematically and stylistically to *Un Homme qui dort:* "Il n'est pas nécessaire que tu sortes de ta maison. Reste à ta table et écoute. N'écoute même pas..." The sudden transformation of the protagonist recalls Joseph K's *Metamorphosis.* The narrator clarifies the relationship: "ce qui te trouble, ce qui t'émeut, ce qui te fait peur, mais qui parfois t'exalte, ce n'est pas la soudaineté de ta métamorphose, c'est au contraire, justement, le sentiment vague et lourd que ce n'en est pas une, que rien n'a changé, que tu as toujours été ainsi..."(30).

The student's sudden *prise de conscience* when confronted by the imposing qualities of a tree necessarily suggests Sartre's Roquentin, whom the narrator associates with yet other alienated heroes: "Quelle merveilleuse invention que l'homme.... Combien d'histoires exaltent ta grandeur, ta souffrance! Combien de Robinson, de Roquentin, de Meursault, de Leverkühn" (156).

Seven pages of the novel are written under the "sign" of Baudelaire (128-34). The section beginning, "Les monstres sont entrés dans ta vie, les rats, tes semblables, tes frères..." describes the multitudes of life's rejects whom the student has come to resemble in his aimlessness. The pages are rich in images of desperation, hideousness, monstrosity—images through which the student wanders in horror. They mirror his degeneracy and attach themselves to him. The encounter of Perec and Baudelaire produces a dazzling catalog of the low life of Paris.

There are incidental allusions to Dostoyevsky (The Grand Inquisitor), Apollinaire ("que vienne la nuit, que sonnent les heures, que les jours s'en aillent, que les souvenirs s'estompent..."—27), Rimbaud ("ton couvert est mis à la table des poètes maudits. Bateau ivre, misérable miracle..."—48), St.-Exupéry (the "aviateur" on page 156) and *Oedipus Rex* (perhaps via Robbe-Grillet: "Le temps qui veille à tout, a donné la solution malgré toi."—162) Another allusion associates the student with one of Perec's favorite literary myths: Melville's Bartleby,[27] whose withdrawal from human affairs leads to a prison death. The final section of Perec's novel emphasizes the distinction, "Tu n'es pas mort." It is perhaps a reproachful comparison with the heroic Bartleby, for the protagonist has gained nothing from his experience, and his future life seems to have little promise.

Before falling into the terrifying despair of the adventure's conclusion, the protagonist experiences briefly an exhilaration which for a short time seems to justify the experiment. He believes that his numbing inner journey has succeeded, for he has gained a mastery of space and at the same time dulled the impact of time upon his life; following his stay in the country he returns to the familiar setting of his room:

> Ta chambre est le centre du monde. Cet antre, ce galetas en soupente qui garde à jamais ton odeur, ce lit où tu te glisses seul, cette étagère, ce linoléum, ce plafond dont tu as compté cent mille fois les fissures, les écailles, les taches, les reliefs, ce lavabo si petit qu'il ressemble à un meuble de poupée, cette bassine, cette fenêtre, ce papier... ces journaux... cette glace fêlée... ces livres rangés, ce radiateur à ailettes... ainsi commence et finit ton royaume, qu'entourent en cercles concentriques, amis ou ennemis, les bruits toujours présents qui te relient seuls au monde... (55-56)

These familiar objects whose extended descriptions make them emanations of his own individuality ("ce papier dont tu connais chaque fleur," "cette glace fêlée qui n'a jamais réfléchi que ton visage"—56) surround him and protect him from the world ("les bruits"). The room which he had earlier described as "ce boyau en soupente qui te sert de chambre" (26), is a fetal paradise which protects and nurtures its occupant. He will later seek to impose upon his life a closed roundness: "Que ta vie soit close, lisse, ronde comme un œuf..." (135). The ideal space of the student's solipsistic fantasy is the womb, which provides a self-sufficient wholeness, a smooth elastic environment without edges or fissures, without beginning or end. It recalls the comforting images of Perec's last published poem,

"L'Eternité"—"Il n'y a plus de déchirure dans l'espace ni dans moi." (See pages 71-72.) But the room is better yet, for it is an obedient environment whose colors and contours are shaped by his perceptions, as in the first pages of the novel when he describes his room as seen through half-closed eyes. What need does he have of any other space when within the designs of his ceiling he can see and describe other realities and fictions as produced by his mind. "Ta chambre est la plus belle des îles désertes, et Paris est un désert que nul n'a jamais traversé. Tu n'as besoin de rien d'autre que de ce calme, que de ce sommeil, que de ce silence, que de cette torpeur" (58). Here in the center of this individualized universe, "maître du monde, petite araignée attentive, au centre de ta toile, tu règnes sur Paris" (61).

This self-sufficient mastery of space, this sensation of shielded contentment and power, is accompanied by a fragile control of the other essential dimension of his existence, time:

> Ton réveil, depuis longtemps, marque cinq heures et quart. Il s'est arrêté pendant ton absence, sans doute, et tu as négligé de le remettre en marche. Dans le silence de ta chambre, le temps ne pénètre plus, il est alentour, bain permanent, encore plus présent, obsédant, que les aiguilles d'un réveil que tu pourrais ne pas regarder, et pourtant légèrement tordu, faussé, un peu suspect: le temps passe, mais tu ne sais jamais l'heure, le clocher de St.-Roch ne distingue pas le quart, ni la demie, ni les trois quarts, l'alternance des feux au croisement de la rue Saint-Honoré et de la rue des Pyramides n'intervient pas chaque minute, la goutte d'eau ne tombe pas chaque minute. Il est dix heures, ou peut-être onze, car comment être sûr que tu as bien entendu, il est tard, il est tôt, le jour naît, la nuit tombe, les bruits ne cessent jamais tout à fait, le temps ne s'arrête jamais totalement, même s'il n'est plus qu'imperceptible: miniscule brèche dans le mur du silence, murmure ralenti, oublié, du goutte à goutte, presque confondu avec les battements de ton cœur. (57-58)

The stopped hands of his clock cannot completely arrest the passage of time. Time surrounds and determinedly penetrates his shelter. Through the small fissures in his protective armor, the visible and audible traces of time reach him obsessively and mark him as surely as the beating of his own heart. The distorted traces of time's passage, inextricably associated with surrounding space, are confused yet pervasive.

Un homme qui dort tient en cercle autour de lui le fil des heures, l'ordre des années et des mondes. Il les consulte d'instinct en s'éveillant et y lit en une seconde le point de la terre qu'il occupe, le temps qui s'est écoulé jusqu'à son réveil; mais leurs rangs peuvent se mêler, se rompre.[28]

Perec's "homme qui dort" shares Proust's fascination with the confused images of time and space which accompany sleep and waking. Four long passages of *Un Homme qui dort* (13-18, 35-40, 89-95, and 111-18) attempt to express the perception of a man as he falls asleep. The four passages interrupt and structure the narrative. The first begins the novel. The presence of the room dominates the protagonist's efforts to fall asleep. Recognizable only because of his familiarity with the room during the day, the objects in the room are fused with the sleeper by the distortions of his line of vision: closing his eyes slightly darkens the images and changes the angle of vision. The images are also distorted by their filtration through his eyelashes and partially blocked by his eyelids. As the room gradually subsides into a grayish uniformity, physical sensations replace vision, the consciousness of the contact between body and bed focuses the sleeper's attention.

The second passage, which precedes the student's departure for his parents' home, carries the description of the sleeper's perceptions a step further. His consciousness tries to deal with the confusing images and words which stream forth from his unconscious memory and impose themselves on his still wakeful mind. These images are not yet dreams, for they appear to the still conscious imagination. Images of playing cards which he tries to arrange, crowds which come and go, walls through which he seeks a hidden passage, forms which appear, enigmatic words and questions, a lake inside his head which he must swim across, all of these images fill his mind until suddenly they vanish, denied, as sleep envelops him in the form of a bubble, a large transparent soap bubble which gradually transforms itself into the shape of his pillow. The worried sleeper fears for a time that he is trapped inside, until "le vrai sommeil" appears to him as long gray beaches, a frozen horizon, and a black sky with gray and white streaks. This comforting image proves unattainable, recedes, as the sleeper turns and wakens.

The third evocation of sleep, which introduces the protagonist's mastery of his studied indifference, portrays a black world upon whose ocean the sleeper sails. The ocean's blackness is interrupted only by the white waves which his passage creates. He sees himself as on the deck of a ship, viewed from two different angles, the images struggling to dominate his perceptions. An impression imposes itself: a painful certainty that the image of the sleeper on the deck of the ship is a real memory, and he must contend with the impossibility and the necessity of this impression. Later the imagery changes, becomes a target, white dots forming a panther's head which grows threateningly and is replaced by a ball of light flying close by.

Through these three passages, actually one long passage presented in three fragments, Perec explores the phenomenon of the passage from wakefulness to sleep, from the sleeper's distorted impressions of his room to purely unconscious dream images. In a sense an elaboration of the passage from Proust, and the product of a fascination with dream imagery which Perec will pursue further in *La Boutique obscure,* these passages are only tangentially related to the novel's plot. The fourth dream passage is different; it follows the protagonist's apparent success in dominating his world. "Le maître anonyme du monde" (108) goes to sleep, and the series of images which assail him lead directly to the disintegration of his protective shell. Very conscious of the physical contact between his body and the sheets and between different parts of his body, he is nonetheless unsure of his exact position and afraid of falling. At the moment when his uncertainty becomes greatest, he is attacked by torturers who stick a sponge full of chalk into his mouth and cotton into his ears. They saw his sinuses, burn his stomach, compress his feet, force a small hat on his head, a narrow coat around his body, strangle him with a necktie, and stuff a knotted cord into his trachea.[29]

The presence of the torturers is despite all reassuring, for after the pain, there is sleep. His body disappears, and he becomes an eye capable of looking inward, with an inescapable intensity:

> Tu te vois, tu te vois te voir, tu te regardes te regarder. Même si tu t'éveillais, ta vision demeurerait identique, immuable. Même si tu parvenais à t'ajouter des milliers, des milliards de paupières, il y aurait encore, derrière, cet œil, pour te voir. Tu ne dors pas, mais le sommeil ne viendra plus. Tu n'es pas éveillé et tu ne te réveilleras jamais. Tu n'es pas mort et la mort même ne saurait te délivrer. (118)

This haunting, inescapable eye, which freezes the protagonist in a state between sleeping and waking, between life and death, introduces his terror, his horror of himself, and the total disillusionment with his indifference.

The last pages of the novel condemn the protagonist's adventure; they express bitter cynicism and scorn for his failure. The second person singular pronoun changes from a friendly intimate companion to a hostile attacker, who ridicules the futility of the protagonist's efforts to isolate himself from humanity.

The ultimate agent of his undoing is time, which despite his efforts and illusions he never really controlled: "Il aurait fallu que le temps s'arrête tout à fait, mais nul n'est assez fort pour lutter contre le temps" (160). "Le temps, qui veille à tout, a donné la solution malgré toi. Le temps, qui connaît la réponse, a continué de couler" (162).

Although the situation in *Un Homme qui dort* is, as Perec explains, diametrically opposed to that of *Les Choses,* the protagonist's failure is similar to the failure of Sylvie and Jérôme, his ultimate plight as unhappy as theirs. He assumed an attitude of superior indifference in order to master time and space by denying them. But time and space, as Jérôme and Sylvie learned, are difficult to control, are impossible to master or ignore. They constitute the absolute limits of the human condition, limits which one must learn to accept and eventually to embrace.

Un Homme qui dort is, like *Les Choses,* a *Bildungsroman* which fizzles. The sleeper, at an even younger age than Jérôme and Sylvie, finds himself at a dead end, alone and resourceless. Neither aloof nor invulnerable nor indifferent, nor even different, he finds himself in the novel's final lines terrifyingly at the mercy of time and space: "Tu n'es plus l'inaccessible, le limpide, le transparent. Tu as peur, tu attends. Tu attends, place Clichy, que la pluie cesse de tomber" (163).[30]

2

THE OULIPIAN NOVELS

La Disparition • *Les Revenentes*

PEREC'S FIRST THREE PUBLISHED NOVELS, *LES CHOSES, QUEL PETIT vélo,* and *Un Homme qui dort,* contain little imaginative storytelling. There is very little plot to *Les Choses* or *Un Homme qui dort;* not much happens, the characters lead unadventurous lives. *Quel petit vélo* tells a story, but a trivial, banal tale, which is ultimately overwhelmed by the style. In all three works, Perec relied on his own experience to furnish the material of his novel and did not attempt to invent creative narrations. As he puts it himself in the postscript of *La Disparition:* [1] "il avait surtout, jusqu'alors, discouru sur sa situation, son moi, son autour social, son adaptation ou son inadaptation…" (309). Perec had not yet become Perec, that is, the inventor of haunting, improbable, imaginative tales. His imagination needed a stimulus; he found it in constraint.

La Disparition began as a game, a challenge, a bet: "Tout partit, tout sortit d'un pari, d'un a priori dont on doutait fort qu'il pût un jour s'ouvrir sur un travail positif" (310). The project of writing a novel without the letter E grew out of Perec's involvement in Oulipo, l'Ouvroir de Littérature Potentielle, a group of writers dedicated to exploring methods of literary creation.[2] In cooperation with writers such as Raymond Queneau, Jacques Roubaud, and Noël Arnaud, Perec studied, developed, and practiced formal constraints which permitted him to develop his literary imagination. As he himself notes, *La Disparition,* his first sustained attempt to write using the techniques of Oulipo, represents a turning point in his literary career: "D'abord lui, qui n'avait pas pour un carat d'inspiration (Il n'y croyait pas, par surcroît, à l'inspiration) il s'y montrait au moins aussi imaginatif qu'un Ponson ou qu'un Paulhan" (310).

The lipogram ("œuvre littéraire dans laquelle on s'astreint à ne pas faire entrer une ou plusieurs lettres de l'alphabet")[3] is not the only formal constraint which Perec employs in *La Disparition*. The text also contains at least one palindrome (a text which can be read forwards or backwards— "Un as noir si mou qu'omis rions à nu."—156), a modified pangram (a sentence using all of the letters of the alphabet; here E is nonetheless exluded—"Portons dix bons whiskys à l'avocat goujat qui fumait au zoo."—55), a procedure borrowed from Raymond Roussel in which a story begins and ends with the same sentence with one letter changed,[4] and the extensive use of quotes, summaries, and allusions from over thirty authors including Mann, Flaubert, Lowry, Hugo, Shakespeare, Musset, Roussel, Mallarmé, Perec, Borges, Poe, and Dostoyevsky. As in Perec's master-work *La Vie mode d'emploi,* one has the impression while reading the novel that the author has included other fanciful word games, and that no one can be aware of them all.

It is certain that it is the constraint of the missing letter E which is the most productive of Perec's techniques in *La Disparition*. One would expect the novel's vocabulary to be impoverished; on the contrary, the reader encounters on every page rare and poetic words.[5] For not only has Perec limited himself to words without E, but one senses that he has attempted to use all of the words in the French language without E, which gives him the opportunity to indulge in one of his favorite literary activities, the creation of catalogs. One finds a catalog of aquatic animals: *pingouins, cormorans, manchots, albatros, rorquals, cachalots, marsouins, dauphins, dugongs, narvals, lamantins;* a catalog of sandwiches, a catalog of gastronomic foods, a catalog of drinks, a catalog of African place names, a catalog of movie stars, a catalog of Napoleonic generals, and others, all without the letter E.

Etienne Lalou, reviewing the novel in *L'Express,*[6] comments on the pleasurable reaction of the reader to Perec's verbal virtuosity:

> On admire le tour de force et savoure les contorsions auxquelles son amusant pari fait se livrer l'auteur. On le guette au tournant. Saura-t-il échapper au piège du "et", et à celui du "le"? On rit quand il traduit "ne faisant ni une ni deux" par "faisant ni six moins cinq ni cinq moins trois", ou "ayant pris mes cliques et mes claques" par "ayant pris mon clic sans avoir pour autant omis mon clac." On apprécie le périphrase

qui fait de Baudelaire "un fils adoptif du commandant Aupick." On applaudit l'auteur lorsqu'il réussit à mettre sur pied un petit texte presque clair d'où le A est banni au même titre qu le E.

(The double lipogram in A and E is actually borrowed from Queneau.) There are several other vocabulary substitutions which deserve to be mentioned: "Un Michaud ou un Pompidou" is a poetry anthology. A "madrigal" is a poem, an "in-folio" a book, a "bristol" a piece of paper, a "pli" a letter. "Kadams," "nagis" and "kouppodoutourams" replace meters or kilometers; and in an elaborate periphrase, the sentence, "Il avait une moustache," becomes "Un fin sillon blafard balafrait son pli labial." All reviewers note the transformations of poems by Mallarmé,[7] Hugo, Baudelaire, and Rimbaud, included in the novel. Other notable *tours de force* include a summary of the novel *Moby Dick,* ending with a *contrepetterie* (Moby Dick, Maudit Bic), a recipe for gefilte fish, passages in English, German, and Japanese, a *blason du corps féminin,* and a tongue-twister.

That this abundance of linguistic creativity could be generated by a disappearance, by an absence, is not inconsistent with contemporary linguistic, philosophical, scientific, and literary speculation: "Le vide, le manque, la coupure... ont reçu valeur de signifié ou ce qui revient au même, de signifiant transcendental: présentation par soi de la vérité (voile/non-voile) comme Logos."[8] Robbe-Grillet cites Einstein and Popper proving that a theory must be flawed to be true, and, referring to Flaubert and Dostoyevsky, concludes, "Des trous se déplaçant dans sa texture, c'est grâce à cela que le texte vit."[9] The flaw, the hole, the disappearance in Perec's text is in itself a powerful linguistic sign which generates the novel's language and imposes itself upon structure and plot.[10]

The constraint which forces Perec to ponder each word, to "abolir tout hasard,"[11] frees him paradoxically from the traditional constraints of the novel:

> Il comprit alors, qu'à l'instar d'un Frank Lloyd Wright construisant sa maison, il façonnait, mutatis mutandi, un produit prototypal qui, s'affranchissant du parangon trop admis qui commandait l'articulation, l'organisation, l'imagination du roman français d'aujourd'hui, abandonnant à tout jamais la psychologisation qui s'alliant à la moralisation constituait pour la plupart l'arc-boutant du bon goût national... (311)

The novel, liberated from the constraints of psychological realism and moral concern becomes a product of pure imagination, building upon itself and the free play of the author's intellectual resources.

In the course of the novel, the absence of the letter E becomes a resonant symbol: "puis, plus tard, s'assurant dans son propos, il donna à sa narration un tour symbolisant qui, suivant d'abord pas à pas la filiation du roman, puis pour finir la constituant, divulguait, sans jamais la trahir tout à fait, la Loi qui l'inspirait" (311). The novel without ever using the letter E refers to it; the absent letter haunts the text,[12] teases and torments the characters, and eventually comes to symbolize something greater than itself, thereby giving the novel a rich network of references—a network that goes beyond the simple game with which the work began.

The novel begins with an *avant-propos* which narrates a series of bloody political upheavals in Paris. The first chapter introduces writer Anton Voyl who, suffering from an unidentifiable malaise, seeks relief in the invention of stories. He "disappears" one day after having sent a cryptic letter to his friends with the almost pangrammatic postscript: "Portons dix bons whiskys à l'avocat goujat qui fumait au zoo." Three of Voyl's friends, responding to the message, meet at the zoo: Amaury Conson, Olga Mavrokhordatos, and Hassan Ibn Abbou. The latter is murdered, and his body disappears. Conson travels to Azincourt to visit Olga who lives on the estate of her father-in-law, Augustus B. Clifford. Olga's husband, Haig Clifford, had died twenty years earlier while singing the role of the commandant in *Don Giovanni*. On the train to Azincourt, Conson meets Arthur Wilburg Savorgnan who is also a friend of Anton Voyl. The night of their arrival, Augustus B. Clifford dies suddenly, uttering the words "Un Zahir." His servant, the Squaw, fills sixty pages explaining the appearance and disappearance of the Zahir, a powerful amulet.

After the Squaw's tale, Olga narrates her life and then dies suddenly. Two police officers, Ottavio Ottaviani and Aloysius Swann are summoned. They arrive to hear Savorgnan's forty-page narration which explains the curse that pursues them all, the family relationships that tie all the characters together, and the vengeance sought against them by "l'intrigant barbu à favoris au poil brun trop touffu."

Savorgnan himself disappears in turn, eliminated by Aloysius Swann, who, working for the "barbu," vaporizes him with a stroke of his Smith-Corona and announces the end of the book. The novel fades into total irreality as the increasingly imaginative tales within tales cancel each

other out and disappear, leaving nonetheless in their wake the impression
that something has occurred.

The novel is obsessed with significant absences. Writer Anton Voyl
is especially troubled by the certainty that something is missing and that the
absence is the source of his malaise. His bookshelf seems to provide a clue:
of the twenty-six volumes in a series, one, number five, is missing (and this
is the first of several repetitions of the same phenomenon, the fifth of
twenty-six elements missing, including chapter five of twenty-six in *La
Disparition*). "Il y avait un manquant. Il y avait un oubli, un blanc, un trou
qu'aucun n'avait vu, n'avait su, n'avait pu, n'avait voulu voir. On avait
disparu. Ça avait disparu" (28).

Voyl is fascinated by the design on a carpet in his room:

> Il s'accroupit sur son tapis, prit son inspiration, fit cinq ou six
> tractions, mais il fatigua trop tôt, s'assit, fourbu, fixant d'un air las
> l'intrigant croquis qui apparaissait ou disparaissait sur l'aubusson
> suivant la façon dont s'organisait la vision:
>
> Ainsi, parfois, un rond, pas tout à fait clos, finissant par un trait
> horizontal: on aurait dit un grand G vu dans un miroir.
>
> Ou, blanc sur blanc, surgissant d'un brouillard cristallin, l'hautain
> portrait d'un roi brandissant un harpon.
>
> Ou, un court instant, sous trois traits droits, l'apparition d'un
> croquis approximatif, insatisfaisant: substituts saillants, contours
> bâtards profilant, dans un vain sursaut d'imagination, la Main à trois
> doigts d'un Sardon ricanant.
>
> Ou, s'imposant soudain, la figuration d'un bourdon au vol lourd,
> portant sur son thorax noir trois articulations d'un blanc quasi lilial.
> (18-19)

This is the first appearance (and disappearance) of the absent E, "un rond
pas tout à fait clos, finissant par un trait horizontal." The intriguing
presence is reinforced by four suggestions of a capital E: "un harpon,"
"trois traits droits," "la Main à trois doigts," and the "trois articulations" on
the bumblebee's thorax (the word *bourdon* which reappears several times in
the text meaning bee or bell is also the typographical term for something left
out). Voyl expects to find in the design of his carpet an answer to his
search:

Il s'irritait. La vision du tapis lui causait un mal troublant. Sous l'amas d'illusions qu'à tout instant son imagination lui dictait, il croyait voir saillir un point nodal, un noyau inconnu qu'il touchait du doigt mais qui toujours lui manquait à l'instant où il allait y aboutir. Il continuait. Il s'obstinait. Fascination dont il n'arrivait plus à s'affranchir. On aurait dit qu'au plus profond du tapis, un fil tramait l'obscur point Alpha, miroir du Grand Tout offrant à foison l'Infini du Cosmos, point primordial d'où surgirait soudain un panorama total, trou abyssal au rayon nul, champ inconnu dont il traçait l'insinuant contour, tourbillon, hauts murs, prison, paroi qu'il parcourait sans jamais la franchir... (20)

Powerful imagery, unaffected by the constraint of the missing letter, expresses Voyl's frustration as he ponders the design's infinite promise and the impenetrable barriers which guard it.

Like a man possessed, Voyl sits in front of the rug, endlessly copying on a piece of paper the motif whose sense eludes him. He draws "trois traits horizontaux (dont l'un au moins paraissait plus court) qu'un grabouillis confus barrait" (55) on the bottom of the letter that he sends to his friends just before his disappearance, a letter in which he expresses his desperate and overwhelming desire to understand the disappearance, the omission, the "grand oubli blanc" which carries him to his death.

Augustus B. Clifford, in the moments preceding his death, experiences a similar torment into which the name of Anton Voyl/voile/voyelle intrudes as a confusing clue:

Midi sonna au carillon. Un bourdon au son lourd, glas ou tocsin, brimbala au loin. Augustus B. Clifford ouvrit un cil. Il avait mal dormi. Il rabâchait sans fin un mot idiot qu'il n'arrivait jamais à saisir: voilà, ou vois-la, ou Voyou ou Voyal? qui, par associations, provoquait un amas, un magma incongru: Substantifs, locutions, slogans, dictons, tout un discours confus, brouillon, dont il croyait à tout instant sortir, mais qui insistait, imposant l'agaçant tourbillon d'un fil vingt fois rompu, vingt fois cousu, mots sans filiation, où tout lui manquait, la prononciation, la transcription, la signification, mais tissant pourtant un flux, un flot continu, compact, clair: impact sûr, intuition, savoir s'incarnant soudain dans un frisson vacillant, dans un flou qu'habitait tout à coup un signal plus sûr, mais qui n'apparaissait qu'un instant pour aussitôt s'abolir. (133)

The absent E makes several other brief appearances throughout the text. In Voyl's retelling of the legend of the Sphinx, the riddle is transformed by his obsession, "Y a-t-il un animal qui ait un corps fait d'un rond pas tout à fait clos finissant par un trait plutôt droit?" (44). Voyl's Oedipus provides a surprisingly apt answer: "Moi."

Albin the Turk (whose name like several others in the novel echoes the "white motif") tattoos the same symbol on the arm of all of his outlaw followers. The sign also appears as a congenital mark on the arms of all of the descendants of a powerful Turkish clan—to which most of the characters belong—and upon Clifford's amulet, the Zahir. Following the death of young Haig Clifford, his father buries him in a corner of his estate, "où, dit-on, poussa alors un gazon blanc figurant grosso modo un croquis aux contours intrigants: harpon à trois dards, ou main à trois doigts, signal maudit du Malin, paraphant au bas d'un manuscrit qu'un Faustillon noircit" (106-07).

The mysterious appearance of the symbol upon Haig's grave associates his death with damnation, the devil, and whiteness. The strange manner of his death reinforces these associations. Three days after his marriage to Olga Mavrokhordatos, Haig, a promising baritone, was singing the role of the Commandant in *Don Giovanni*. In the final act when the statue of the commandant responds to Don Juan's mocking invitation and summons him to their infernal encounter, Haig made his entrance too soon, encased in a white stucco statue. Disoriented, he fell and was killed. The narrator's preface to the account of his death emphasizes the fatal principle which caused it:

> Oui, ami qui nous lis, tu voudrais, toi aussi, qu'ici tout soit fini. Douglas Haig Clifford s'unit à Olga Mavrokhordatos; ils connaîtront l'amour, la paix, l'amical unisson. Ils auront vingt-six bambins, tous survivront.
>
> Las, non! souhait trop hardi! il n'y aura pas d'absolution. Nul Tout-Puissant n'offrira son pardon à Douglas Haig. La Damnation qui partout, qui toujours, parcourt l'obscur signal qu'à l'infini ma main voudrait approfondir, accomplira ici aussi son fatum. La mort qui, trois jours plus tard, faisant son irruption à Urbino, annonçait, vingt ans plus tard, la disparition d'Anton Voyl, la disparition d'Hassan Ibn Abbou... (104-05)

The death of young Haig appears to be the result of the convergence of several different curses. The narrator attributes his death to the damnation which follows all of the characters in the novel. His father is persuaded that his death is the result of the curse of the Zahir which as a child Haig had stolen from his father and fed to his pet fish. (The message of the Zahir's curse has appeared mysteriously in white letters on Clifford's billiard table which Anton Voyl deciphered just hours before Haig's death.) Haig's marriage to Olga brought down upon him the curse of the Turkish warrior Albin among whose descendants Olga was thought to be. Actually, as Arthur Wilburg Savorgnan ultimately reveals, Haig and Olga were doubly cursed, for they were brother and sister, fathered by Savorgnan himself, and subject therefore to the terrible vengeance of their grandfather, "l'intrigant barbu à favoris au poil brun trop touffu," who, for years, pursued his two sons, Savorgnan and Amaury Conson, and all of their children, including not only Haig and Olga, but also Anton Voyl and Hassan Ibn Abbou.

Olga dies at Azincourt, barely articulating the word "malediction," after she had cut open Haig's pet fish and found the Zahir. The horrified witnesses to her death attribute it and her dying word to a sudden understanding of the power of the Zahir. Savorgnan understands the word differently: "Pour moi, il s'agit d'un trauma maladif, un anthrax, ou plutôt un mal blanc s'attaquant aux cordons vocaux, impliquant constriction ou fluxoin, banissant ou tout au moins troublant la diction, d'où son nom" (215). Asked to elaborate this theory of Olga's death, Savorgnan theorizes a more subtle form of damnation which pursues the characters:

> L'on a cru qu'Anton, ou qu'Augustus, avait connu la mort sans pouvoir s'ouvrir du torturant tracas qui l'assaillait. Mais non! Il a connu la mort pour n'avoir pu, pour n'avoir su s'ouvrir, pour n'avoir pas rugi l'insignifiant son qui aurait à jamais, aussitôt, aboli la Saga où nous vagissons. Car nous avons construit, nous taisant, un Talion qui nous poursuit aujourd'hui; nous avons tu la damnation, nous n'avons pas dit son nom, lors nous punit la Damnation dont nous ignorons tout: Nous avons connu, nous connaîtrons la Mort, sans jamais pouvoir la fuir, sans jamais savoir pourquoi nous mourrons, car, issus d'un Tabou dont nous nommons l'autour sans jamais l'approfondir jusqu'au bout (souhait vain, puisqu'aussitôt dit, aussitôt transcrit, il abolirait l'ambigu pouvoir du discours où nous survivons), nous tairons toujours

la Loi qui nous agit, nous laissant croupir, nous laissant mourir dans
l'Indivulgation qui nourrit sa propagation... (216)

Savorgnan's explanation of the true nature of their damnation is a
remarkably lucid description of the fictional universe which imprisons and
condemns them. Amaury Conson, persuaded by Savorgnan's theory,
compares the improbable adventures which beset them to the imaginative
fabulations of a crazy author who prefers gratuitous and instinctive plot
incidents to a consistent and continuous development. Savorgnan responds
that this is the nature of the modern novel which paradoxically finds the
inspiration for such unlimited play of the imagination through the creation of
arduous constraints: "Il faut, sinon, il suffit, qu'il n'y ait pas un mot qui
soit fortuit, qui soit dû au pur hasard... qu'a contrario tout mot soit produit
sous la sanction d'un tamis contraignant, sous la sommation d'un canon
absolu!" (217).

This conversation is one of several metaliterary discussions through
which the novel justifies itself. Anton Voyl, the novel's first victim, is a
writer. In his journal, in his reflections on the carpet, and in his discussion
of the writing on the billiard table, Voyl expresses his admiration for certain
works of literature, certain literary themes, and certain techniques, which
are specifically the sources, themes, and techniques of *La Disparition* (pp.
112, 41, and 195-96). Amaury Conson, pondering Voyl's words, shares
his intuition that the solution to their predicament is literary:

> Il s'irritait, n'arrivait plus à saisir l'insinuant fil qui tissait son
> association. Un roman? Anton Voyl n'avait-il pas dit un jour qu'un
> roman donnait la solution? Un flot brouillon, tourbillonnant d'imagi-
> nations s'imposa soudain à lui: *Moby Dick?* Malcolm Lowry? *La
> Saga du Non-A*, par Van Vogt? Ou, vus dans un miroir, trois six sur
> l'immaculation du dos d'un Christian Bourgois? Ou l'obscur Signal
> d'Inclusion, main à trois doigts qu'imprimait Roubaud sur un
> Gallimard? *Blanc ou l'Oubli*, d'Aragon? *Un Grand Cri Vain? La
> Disparition?*[13] (220)

Voyl and Conson are of course absolutely correct. The source of their
damnation is the Grand Cri Vain (grand écrivain), author of *La Disparition*,
"l'intrigant barbu à favoris au poil brun trop touffu," who pursues
relentlessly the characters of the novel, forcing upon them his vengeance,

his terrible law, which imprisons them within a strange fiction that they struggle to understand.

Like the athletes in Perec's other novel of disappearance, *W ou le souvenir d'enfance*,[14] the characters perform in a world whose rules they do not know. They try to play according to the rules that they do know (here, the models of the detective or curse novel) only to find that they are locked inside a capricious, arbitrary system which punishes them and squashes their every effort to understand why. This sobering reflection on a novel which was intended to entertain and amuse undoubtedly came to Perec himself who ends his summary on the novel's back cover:

> Qui sont ces êtres qui disparaissent et quel est le secret qu'ils emportent dans leur tombe? Nous ne le saurons jamais, mais au moins saurons-nous qu'il les fit vivre et qu'il les fit mourir et que le livre entier n'est que l'exacte trace de cette damnation sans fin.

Confronted with his own totalitarian creation, Perec, with gentle irony, pities the fate of his victims and points to the book as a "trace" of their lives and deaths. Ewa Pawlikowska demonstrates the importance of the notion of "trace" in the works of Perec; for her, the tendency to leave traces, to show and to hide simultaneously, translated by the dual (and palindromatic) opposition *trace/écart* (Derrida's *voile/non-voile*) "se trouve à l'origine de l'écriture de Perec."[15] In *W ou le souvenir d'enfance,* Perec himself uses the notion of "trace" to explain his writing, referring to the life and death of his parents, his father killed in the war, his mother in a Nazi death camp, "J'écris parce qu'ils ont laissé en moi leur marque indélébile et que la trace en est l'écriture."[16]

Perec's summary with its ironic concern that the book serve as a monument to the victims of his own repressive system relates the seemingly superficial game with which the novel originated to his most profound personal obsessions. His emergence in *La Disparition* as an original, imaginative storyteller springs from the discovery of constraint. Perec becomes Perec as the result of two resonant creative forces: on the one hand the virtuosity and joy in playing games; on the other, the personal experience, the scars left by the deaths of his parents. It is in *La Disparition* that for the first time the two forces meet. The game with which the project began, unconsciously but inevitably, engenders the totalitarian system which destroys the characters. Perec's reflection on the back cover reveals his recognition of the parallel courses of the horror he survived and the system he has created. The novel transcends the game with which it began because of Perec's will that his characters struggle heroically though vainly against their imprisoning system, against their own disappearance, and leave a trace of their passage.

• • •

Taking the challenge he had faced in *La Disparition* one step further, Perec in 1972 published *Les Revenentes*,[17] a 114-page novel whose only vowel is E. The difficulties are awesome, and ultimately Perec received from his Oulipian colleagues authorization, voted March 7, 1972, to take certain liberties: "qu" is written "q" (qel, qe, qerelle, qelqe, etc.), and certain spelling distortions (as for example in the novel's title), "seront plus ou moins progressivement admis au cours du texte" (9).

On the novel's back cover, Perec hypothesizes a third novel which would complete the series begun with *La Disparition* and *Les Revenentes:* the first uses words that contain no E; the second uses a completely different set of words which contain E and no other vowel. Missing from both novels are all of the words in the language which contain E and at least one other vowel. For Perec, the challenge of writing a novel using only that set of words appears relatively trivial.

Perec also points out that although *La Disparition* and *Les Revenentes* do not have a single word in common, they resemble one another in several ways. *Les Revenentes* is an imaginative police story, full of strange adventures, including an African assassination. It begins in the style of the *roman noir,* perhaps as interpreted by San-Antonio; the last chapters, the most sexually explicit in the published works of Perec, are strongly reminiscent of Sade's *Philosophie dans le boudoir.* Other recognizable "sources" are Marcel Proust and the Robert Dictionary, for as in *La Disparition,* the vocabulary includes rare and obscure words chosen for their charm and their vocalic limitations.

The plot is much simpler than that of *La Disparition,* the action is remarkably unified. A beautiful young woman, Bérengère de Brémen-Brevert, seeks, with the help of her friend the Bishop of Exeter, to sell her jewels. The first person narrator, Clément, with the help of his sister Estelle, her friend Hélène, and Bérengère's pupil Thérèse, plans to steal the jewels. Clément kills several members of a rival gang also interested in the jewels and concludes a treaty with the gang's leader, Ernest, whereby they agree to work together and split the profits. All of the characters participate in a forty-page orgy with the almost impotent Bishop and several priests. Clément and his cohorts overcome the treachery of Ernest and his gang and escape with the jewels.

The novel begins in almost flawless French:

> Telles des chèvres en détresse, sept Mercédès-Benz vertes, les fenêtres crêpées de reps grège, descendent lentement West End Street et prennent sénestrement Temple Street vers les vertes venelles semées de hêtres et de frênes près desqelles se dresse, svelte et empesé en même temps, l'Evêché d'Exeter. Près de l'entrée des thermes, des gens s'empressent. (13)

Only the authorized "desqelles" varies from acceptable usage. Nothing in the text stands out as illogical or impossible. That a building could be *svelte* and *empesé* is unusual but imaginable. The opening simile is rather fanciful: a goatlike Mercedes is hard to visualize. But the passage is clear, descriptive, reasonably correct, and interesting; and it effectively reproduces, while slightly parodying it, the style of the *roman noir*.

Several other passages stand out as examples of artistic mastery of an impossible medium; in one, the narrator expresses his nostalgia for the Canadian Arctic:

> Le spleen me prend et me berce. Je rêve de mes terres d'Ellesmere. Ses mers et ses grèves, et les tétrels, et les tempêtes. Se déprendre! Etre en mes terres! Et cette netteté céleste qe l'éther reflète, et le grès des crêtes et le blé des prés ensemencé dès septembre! (23)

The simplicity of the expression, the sharpness of the images and the rhythmic effect produced by the repeated "et," translating the obsessive nature of the related details, creates a moving poetic effect. Another exemplary text describes the entrance of Clément's scantily dressed assistants:

> Belles telles les déesses éternelles de l'été, telles des Eve qe les serpents ne cessent de tenter, Estelle, Thérèse et Hélène, qe vêtent des prétextes de crêpe tellement légère qe le vent les relève fréqemment et révèlent les ventre et les fesses, entrent. (77)

The novel is a remarkable tour de force containing other notable passages such as the description of the low-life of Exeter's Needle Street and, of course, the hetero- and homosexual couplings of priests and gangsters. It deserves and has received scant recognition as a work of art. It deserves rather to be recognized, like Perec's 5,000 word palindrome,[18] and other contributions to Oulipo publications,[19] as an incredible feat of entertaining linguistic virtuosity.

3

THE AUTOBIOGRAPHICAL WORKS

W ou le souvenir d'enfance • *La Boutique obscure* • *Espèces d'espaces* • *Je me souviens*

IN THE ARTICLE, "NOTES SUR CE QUE JE CHERCHE,"[1] PEREC LISTS AS his autobiographical works *W ou le souvenir d'enfance, La Boutique obscure, Je me souviens,* and other incidental pieces such as "Lieux où j'ai dormi." But he goes on to add, "...aucun de mes livres n'échappe tout à fait à un certain marquage autobiographique." Anne Roche[2] includes among his autobiographical works *Un Homme qui dort, Récits d'Ellis Island,* and *Un Cabinet d'amateur.* I have excluded from this chapter those three works, which I discuss elsewhere, and I include *Espèces d'espaces,* whose autobiographical importance seems evident.

In *W ou le souvenir d'enfance,*[3] Perec weaves together two narratives, an attempted autobiography and a recreated childhood fantasy, into a rich literary tapestry which has fascinated readers and earned the appreciation of critics as a major literary work.[4] Bernard Pingaud considers it "l'oeuvre la plus énigmatique de Perec, celle aussi où il se livre le plus et qui appelle irrésistiblement le commentaire."[5]

Superficially the weaving is rather a coarse grafting with obvious seams, for Perec merely alternates chapters of the two narratives. One of the narratives tells the story of Gaspard Winckler, his missing namesake, and his fascination with an Island in the Tierra del Fuego dominated by athletic competition. The other narrative represents Perec's attempt to piece together memories and reminders of his childhood. The final chapter quotes at length from David Rousset's *L'Univers concentrationnaire* [6] to emphasize the most obvious relationship between autobiography and fantasy.

There is a further weaving which takes place, a more subtle creation of intertextual relationships which bind the two narratives to create a complex whole which is greater than the sum of its parts, and which has inspired remarkably diverse interpretations: as a condemnation of the capitalist system,[7] as an oedipal search for identity,[8] and as an affirmation of Jewish identity and an allegory of PLO fanatacism.[9]

Perec's project is self-consciously literary: "Le projet d'écrire mon histoire s'est formé en même temps que mon projet d'écrire" (41). As proof, he offers two autobiographical passages, written years earlier, which, like Proust's description of the "clochers de Martinville" demonstrate an early interest in the literary preservation of childhood memories.

Literary antecedents of the novel's form abound: J.-B. Baronian mentions Faulkner's *The Wild Palms;*[10] Dickens in *Bleak House* and Beckett in *Molloy* also join together what seems at first to be unrelated texts. Other writers mentioned in discussions of the novel's form include Kafka, Verne, Leiris and of course Queneau, whom Perec quotes in epigraphs to the first and second parts of the novel. In the autobiographical sections, Perec mentions in addition his readings of Flaubert and Roussel, and Gaspard Winckler compares himself to Melville's Ishmael and Bartleby.

One other significant and perhaps unconscious literary precedent needs to be mentioned at this point. In the second chapter which serves as a belated preface, Perec refers to the two strands, "Mais dans le réseau qu'ils tissent comme dans la lecture que j'en fais, je sais que se trouve inscrit et décrit le chemin que j'ai parcouru, le cheminement de mon histoire, et l'histoire de mon cheminement" (14). The insistence on the notion of "chemin" recalls Dante's "Nel mezzo del camin di nostra vita." Perec at age 38, with every reason to believe he was but in the middle of his *chemin,* stops to meditate upon his past and the light it may throw upon his future. The two quotes from Queneau reflect this intention:

> Cette brume insensée où s'agitent des ombres, comment pourrais-je l'éclaircir?
> Cette brume insensée ou s'agitent des ombres, —est-ce donc là mon avenir?

Consciously at a crossroads, Perec seizes upon the doubleness of the route going before and after and constructs a book based on doubling with the X as a major symbol:

A côté de la villa, à l'autre côté de la route, il y avait une ferme... occupée par un vieil homme aux moustaches grises... et dont je garde un souvenir net: il sciait son bois sur un chevalet formé de deux croix parallèles, prenant appui sur l'extrémité de leurs deux montants de manière à former cette figure en X que l'on appelle "Croix de Saint-André," et réunies par une traverse perpendiculaire, l'ensemble s'appelant, tout bonnement un X.

Mon souvenir n'est pas souvenir de la scène, mais souvenir du mot, seul souvenir de cette lettre devenue mot, de ce substantif unique dans la langue à n'avoir qu'une lettre unique, unique aussi en ceci qu'il est le seul à avoir la forme de ce qu'il désigne... mais signe aussi du mot rayé nul—la ligne des X sur le mot que l'on n'a pas voulu écrire—, signe contradictoire de l'ablation... et de la multiplication, de la mise en ordre (axe des X) et de l'inconnu mathématique, point de départ enfin d'une géométrie fantasmique dont le V dédoublé constitue la figure de base et dont les enchevêtrements multiples tracent les symboles majeurs de l'histoire de mon enfance: deux V accolés par leurs pointes dessinent un X; en prolongeant les branches du X par des segments égaux et perpendiculaires, on obtient une croix gammée (卐) elle-même facilement décomposable par une rotation de 90° d'un des segments en ⟩ sur son coude inférieur en signe ⟩⟩ ; la superposition de deux V tête-bêche aboutit à une figure (XX) dont il suffit de réunir horizontalement les branches pour obtenir une étoile juive (✡). (105-06)

This complex network of associations, this "géométrie fantasma-gorique," probably contemporary to the original elaboration of *W* and which groups symbols of words crossed out, removal, multiplication, the unknown quantity, Nazism, the gestapo, and Judaism with our original evocation of X as a crossroad, is part of the unifying substructure upon which Perec has built his book of memoirs.

Robert Misrahi[11] has analyzed the structural relationships of the different parts of the book, specifically the doubling and mirroring effects. He divides the book into four parts which can be schematized as follows:

I	II
W1	W2
P1	P1

The W sections tell the story of Winckler and the Island W. The P sections are Perec's memoirs. Parts I and II of the novel are divided by titles ("Première partie," "Deuxième partie"), by an ellipsis, "(...)," on page 85 and by the Queneau quotes.

In W1 Gaspard Winckler narrates his meeting with Otto Apfelstahl who enjoins him to search the islands of the Tierra del Fuego for the original Gaspard Winckler, a sickly child whose name and passport the second Gaspard Winckler received from a pacifist group following his desertion from the army, and who had been a passenger on a shipwrecked yacht. W2 is Winckler's description of the Island W whose society of athletes he explains at great length. The reader assumes that Winckler discovered this island while searching for his namesake, but there is not the slightest allusion in W2 to the search or to any of the events of W1.

In P1 Perec, who was born in 1936, insists on his lack of real memories of his prewar childhood. His descriptions of his parents, father killed in battle, mother dead at Auschwitz, are based on photos and information provided by relatives. P2 contains his memories of the war years, following his flight to Villard-de-Lans in the Alps, and of his return to Paris after the war. These memories are personal, but isolated and floating: "Désormais, les souvenirs existent, fugaces ou tenaces, futiles ou pesants, mais rien ne les rassemble" (93).

Gaspard Winckler's search for his namesake, the sickly child lost at sea or perhaps abandoned by his mother, introduces a detective motif which is common to the first halves of both narratives. The parallels between the investigation of the disappearance of Gaspard Winckler and Perec's search through old photographs and documents for evidence of the orphaned boy he once was and doesn't remember are obvious and disturbing. Claude

Burgelin[12] like Perec himself (59) speaks of Oedipus, and like Philippe Berthier[13] notes that both Perec's and Winckler's mothers are named Cécile. Both narrators use similar language to describe their searches:

> Je n'ai pour étayer mes souvenirs improbables que le secours de photos jaunies, de témoignages rares et de documents dérisoires. (P, 21-22)

> Longtemps j'ai cherché les traces de mon histoire, consulté des cartes et les annuaires, des monceaux d'archives. (W, 10)

There exist other, incidental, links between the two stories. In both, the city of Venice is the site of a sudden memory (perhaps an allusion to Proust):

> Il y a ___ ans, à Venice, dans une gargote de la Giudecca, j'ai vu entrer un homme que j'ai cru reconnaître. (W, 10)

> Il y a sept ans, un soir à Venise, je me souvins tout à coup que cette histoire s'appelait "W" et qu'elle était, d'une certaine façon, sinon l'histoire du moins une histoire de mon enfance. (P, 14)

In the fifth chapter, Gaspard Winckler waits in a bar for Apfelstahl and is approached by a waiter:

> —Voulez-vous des bretzels?
> —Pardon, fis-je, sans comprendre.
> —Des bretzels. Des bretzels pour manger en buvant votre bière.
> —Non, merci. Je ne mange jamais de bretzels. (26)

This bizarre insistence on the repetition of the word "bretzel" is perhaps related to an autobiographical passage:

> Le nom de ma famille est Peretz. Il se trouve dans la Bible. En hébreu, cela veut dire "trou," en russe "poivre," en hongrois (à Budapest, plus précisément), c'est ainsi que l'on désigne ce que nous appelons "Bretzel" ("Bretzel" n'est d'ailleurs rien d'autre qu'un diminutif [Bretzele] de Beretz, comme Baruk ou Barek, est forgé sur la même racine que Peretz—en arabe, sinon en hébreu, B et P sont une seule et même lettre.) (51)

One other incidental use of similar language should be noted:

> Dans le témoignage que je m'apprête à faire, je fus témoin, et non acteur. Je ne suis pas le héros de mon histoire. (W, 10)
> L'événement eut lieu, un peu plus tard ou un peu plus tôt, et je n'en fus pas la victime héroïque mais un simple témoin. (P, 109)

The structural similarities between the first half of P and the first half of W seem clear and intentional. A similar parallel cannot be convincingly demonstrated in the second half of the book. In fact, the second half of W doesn't even refer to its own first half. The elaborate and at first scientific (ethnological) description of the athletic training, competition, and hierarchy of the island comes to assume an independent life of its own, leaving only one indirect and uncertain shadow upon its autobiographical counterpart. Perec describes his love of skiing (139-41) in terms which echo W: "apprentissage approfondi," "skis écartés en V," "au sommet de la hiérarchie," "un protocole apparemment immuable," "risque de fracture grave... les chances de performances exceptionnelles." This section of the autobiography includes a violent sports-related episode: an angry boy strikes Perec with a ski, cutting his lip and breaking two teeth.

There exists in the description of the athletic system of W a further fragmentation of the text, for there are two opposing visions of the way of life. The first descriptions are purely geographic and historic. The first allusions to the athletic system seem positive: "Qui ne serait enthousiasmé par cette discipline audacieuse, par ces prouesses quotidiennes, cette lutte au coude à coude, cette ivresse que donne la victoire?" (92). But beginning with chapter XVIII (119), the evolution of the text becomes apparent: an increasingly subjective and ultimately scandalized narrator begins to reveal the horrible, the barbaric, and the despotic facts of life on W. Losers are routinely deprived of their evening meal; often their punishment is more severe; in extreme cases they are stoned to death. The sports officials introduce unknown and arbitrary handicaps, injustices which give them the ultimate right to decide who wins or loses. At an annual competition, the women of the island are set naked upon the playing field to be pursued and raped by the male athletes who are cheered on by the spectators. During the first six months of their apprenticeship, children are chained hand and foot and often gagged. Old athletes are deprived of all rights and forced to find food in garbage cans or to eat the decaying bodies of executed losers.[14]

The final chapter of W is a forceful and derisive condemnation of the tyrannical system and the plight of those trapped within it, which clearly associates W with Nazi death camps:

> L'athlète W n'a guère de pouvoir sur sa vie. Il n'a rien à attendre du temps qui passe. Ni l'alternance des jours et des nuits ni le rythme des saisons ne lui seront d'aucun secours.... Il faut les voir, ces athlètes squelettiques, au visage terreux, à l'échine toujours courbée, ces crânes chauves et luisants, ces yeux pleins de panique, ces plaies purulentes, toutes ces marques indélébiles d'une terreur sans fond.... Il faut voir fonctionner cette machine énorme dont chaque rouage participe, avec une efficacité implacable, à l'anéantissement systématique des hommes, pour ne plus trouver surprenante la médiocrité des performances enregistrées: le 100 mètres se court en 23" 4, le 200 mètres en 51"; le meilleur sauteur n'a jamais dépassé 1,30m. (216-18)

On the back cover of the book, Perec calls attention to the discontinuity of his work, focusing not on the alternation between W and P, but rather on the break between the two halves of W:

> Le récit d'adventures, à côté, a quelque chose de grandiose, ou peut-être de suspect. Car il commence par raconter une histoire et, d'un seul coup, se lance dans une autre: dans cette rupture, cette cassure qui suspend le récit autour d'on ne sait quelle attente, se trouve le lieu initial d'ou est sorti ce livre, ces *points de suspension* auxquels se sont accrochés les fils rompus de l'enfance et la trame de l'écriture.

Perec emphasizes the phrase, *"points de suspension"* which refers specifically to the ellipsis on the otherwise blank page 85. This break in the text, this blank page—which Burgelin[15] compares to the Brechtian technique of distantiation used to reduce pathetic emotional impact—is central to Perec's conception of his book: "le lieu initial d'où est sorti ce livre." Anne Roche summarizes the meaning of the blank page in terms of the two interrupted narratives:[16]

> S'il était licite de se hasarder à noircir cette page blanche, on pourrait dire que, dans cet espace où rien n'est dit, le faux Gaspard Winckler part pour W et le petit Georges Perec part pour Villard, quittant sa mère qu'il ne reverra jamais (elle mourra à Auschwitz). En fait, dans cette

page blanche, c'est l'explosion de l'univers (fictif pour Winckler, "réel" pour Perec), qui *fonde* le texte.

Page 85, "cette page blanche... cet espace où rien n'est dit," this "rupture," this "cassure," represents on one hand a perfectly neutral ground, a suspension, in Perec's geometric terms the crossing points of the two axes (x=0, y=0). On the other hand, it is ground zero, "l'explosion de l'univers," the point of intersection of "une enfance traversée par la guerre."[17] It has the same value as the page inserted by Victor Hugo between the second and third poems of the Fourth Book of *Les Contemplations,* bearing the date "4 Septembre 1843" and a series of "points de suspension" to mark for the bereaved poet the before and after of the death of his beloved daughter, his silence, and the eventual conception of the book of poems.

Perec relates the notion of *suspension* directly to his departure for Villard. His vague memory of the departure includes three details: his mother had given him a Charlie Chaplin comic book on whose cover Chaplin is floating from a parachute attached to his suspenders. Perec's arm was in a sling, or (because his aunt denies the presence of a sling) he was wearing a bandage for a hernia, a "suspensoir." Perec analyzes these uncertain details:

> Un triple trait parcourt ce souvenir: parachute, bras en écharpe, bandage herniaire: cela tient de la prothèse. Pour être besoin d'étai. Seize ans plus tard, en 1958, lorsque les hasards du service militaire ont fait de moi un éphémère parachutiste, je pus lire, dans la minute même du saut, un texte déchiffré de ce souvenir: je fus précipité dans le vide; tous les fils furent rompus; je tombai, seul et sans soutien. Le parachute s'ouvrit. La corolle se déploya, fragile et sûr suspens avant la chute maîtrisée. (77)

The "texte déchiffré de ce souvenir" is Perec's belated understanding of the "obsessive metaphor" related to his departure. In response to his own questioning ("Je ne sais où se sont brisés les fils qui me rattachent à mon enfance."—21), he discovers sixteen years later the sensation of the repressed childhood anguish: "je fus précipité dans le vide; tous les fils furent rompus; je tombai, seul et sans soutien." The ties to his childhood were severed irrevocably ("Je n'ai pas d'autre choix que d'évoquer ce que trop longtemps j'ai nommé l'irrévocable."—22) at the Gare de Lyon when he was thrown into the emptiness of the train, exiled and orphaned in one traumatic moment, which his childhood imagination buries under images of suspension.

Despite his perception of the pathos of the repressed memory, Perec refuses to dwell upon it. He presents one subtly restrained image, in the conditional perfect, of what life might have been with his mother (95); but more interesting to Perec is to observe and analyze the birth of his artistic imagination through his unconscious attempts to adjust to the loss of his mother. With remarkable lucidity, he continues to explore the notions of "cassure" and "rupture" as they reappear in his life as a series of dislocations, first of all of his memories:

> Ils sont comme cette écriture non liée, faite de lettres isolées incapables de se souder entre elles pour former un mot, qui fut la mienne jusqu'à l'âge de dix-sept ou dix-huit ans, ou comme ces desseins dissociés, disloqués, dont les éléments épars ne parvenaient presque jamais à se relier les uns aux autres, et dont, à l'époque de W, entre, disons, ma onzième et ma quinzième années, je couvris des cahiers entiers:

> Personnages que rien ne rattachait au sol qui était censé les supporter, navires dont les voilures ne tenaient pas aux mâts, ni les mâts à la coque, machines de guerre, engins de mort, aéroplanes et véhicules aux mécanismes improbables, avec leurs tuyères déconnectés, leurs filins interrompus, leurs roues tournant dans le vide; les ailes des avions se détachaient du fuselage, les jambes des athlètes étaient séparées des troncs, les bras séparés des torses, les mains n'assuraient aucune prise. (93)

This catalog of effects, this rich network of obsessive imagery relating notions of suspension, dislocation, and fracture becomes part of Perec's creative imagination, from which will spring a fascination with puzzles (cf, *La Vie mode d'emploi,* as well as his poetry and crossword puzzles published in *Télérama* and *Le Point),* with missing elements (*La Disparition,* written without the letter E, *Les Revenentes* written without all of the other vowels) and with the notion of "coupure" (the word recurs hauntingly in Perec's explanation of the Ellis Island experience in the film, "Récits d'Ellis Island"; it is also an element of Sylvie and Jérôme's flight to Tunisia in *Les Choses).*

An additional personal anecdote and Perec's interpretation of it further relate these associated images to the childhood separation. He remembers in the spring of 1942, "bien qu'elle soit chronologiquement impossible"(108), a sledding accident, a broken shoulder blade and his right hand tied behind his back in a sling, which earned for him much consoling pity. Later information convinces Perec that the accident actually happened to another boy:

> L'événement eut lieu un peu plus tard ou un peu plus tôt, et je n'en fus pas la victime mais un simple témoin. Comme pour le bras en écharpe de la gare de Lyon, je vois bien ce que pouvaient remplacer ces fractures éminemment réparables qu'une immobilisation temporaire suffisait à réduire, même si la métaphore, aujourd'hui, me semble inopérante pour décrire ce qui avait été cassé et qu'il était sans doute vain d'espérer enfermer dans le simulacre d'un membre fantôme. Plus simplement, ces thérapeutiques imaginaires, moins contraignantes que tutoriales, ces points de suspension, désignaient des douleurs nommables et venaient à point justifier des cajoleries dont les raisons réelles n'étaient données qu'à voix basse. (109-10)

The memory of the reparable fracture, recognized by the mature Perec as an "inoperative" metaphor for a more traumatic and irreparable break in his life, requires the imaginary sling, the healing suspension which binds the wound (Matthieu Galey refers to the book as "des Mémoires en charpie"[18]). The real wound, only whispered and not fully understood by the child, is the absence, the silence, which steals his mother from him.

The absence itself explodes within Perec's imagination; the mature Perec's recognition of the source and role of his broken and suspended imagery has, in Anne Roche's terms, founded the text. Alain Poirson, speaking of the parallel investigations of Winckler and Perec, finds, "Dans l'un et l'autre cas, l'enquêteur ne trouve pas son autre, mais découvre ce qu'il ne cherchait pas: Perec l'écriture, le second l'univers concentrationnaire."[19] Perec himself expresses the relationship between his experience and his need to write about it:

> J'aurais beau traquer mes lapsus...ou rêvasser pendant deux heures sur la longueur de la capote de mon papa, ou chercher dans mes phrases, pour évidemment les trouver aussitôt, les résonances mignonnes de l'œdipe ou de la castration, je ne retrouverais jamais, dans mon ressassement,

que l'ultime reflet d'une parole absente à l'écriture, le scandale de leur silence et de mon silence: je n'écris pas pour dire que je ne dirai rien, je n'écris pas pour dire que je n'ai rien à dire. J'écris: j'écris parce que nous avons vécu ensemble, parce que j'ai été un parmi eux, ombre au milieu de leurs ombres, corps près de leur corps, j'écris parce qu'ils ont laissé en moi leur marque indélébile et que la trace en est l'écriture; leur souvenir est mort à l'écriture; l'écriture est le souvenir de leur mort et l'affirmation de ma vie. (59)

Perec finds reflections of the "parole absente à l'écriture" in his childhood memories, in the working of his imagination, and in his genetic and psychological structure. These reflections constitute the form and imagery of his book of memoirs. To present the splintered images of a shattered childhood, Perec employs a form which mirrors its content and which calls forth associated images which have accompanied him since the childhood experiences the book evokes. The book is for Perec an essential effort to accept his past and to affirm his present and future by assuming the responsibility of memorializing his lost parents and subsequently lost childhood.

"Ma mère n'a pas de tombe" (57). The journey to W, into the horrors of the imaginary fascist universe, and the literary description of that journey, which accompanies the evocation of the missing tomb and the irrevocable departure from the Gare de Lyon, are a monument to the absent parents—a monument that fills the scandalous silence and binds the painful fracture.

•   •   •

La Boutique Obscure,[20] Perec's description of 120 of his dreams (plus four dreams by other people), was conceived as a literary project, the putting into words[21] of images and emotions which he dreamed from May 1968 to August 1972. The volume also includes a thematic index and a postface by Roger Bastide which relates Perec's work to the sociological orientation of the publisher, *Cause Commune.*

Claude Bonnefoy, reviewing the book in *Nouvelles Littéraires,*[22] compares Perec's project with those of others who have explored dreams: surrealists, psychoanalysts, and ethnographers. He finds that the nature of Perec's dreams justifies Bastide's sociological conclusion that the dreams of Perec represent, "une réponse à une certaine situation sociale."[23] For

Bonnefoy, "les rêves de Pérec (sic) reflètent, transposent d'une manière fort lisible, les préoccupations, désirs, espoirs, inquiétudes de sa vie quotidienne. Son travail, ses amis, ses chats, l'argent y tiennent une place importante." Both Bonnefoy and Bastide find that missing from Perec's dreams are the traditional, analyzable symbols of sexual repression, which have been replaced by a new preoccupation, "En bref, maintenant puisque le sexuel est libre, c'est le refoulement de la protestation et de la contestation politique qui remplace le refoulement érotique."[24]

Ignoring the intentional misinterpretation of the notion of *refoulement,* one can agree that in these texts Perec emerges as "un amoureux plutôt comblé."[25] And it is also true that his dreams are haunted by images of political repression. The fear of arrest recurs frequently: in four dreams Perec is a prisoner in a concentration camp; in several others, the SS, the CRS, the police, and even Adolph Hitler appear, constituting a threatening presence. To what extent these nightmares of a reality which Perec knew only indirectly, referring to events which marked him between his fourth and ninth years, can be classified "sociological" seems debatable. It is much more probable that these scenes are reflections of the childhood scars whose repression Perec explores in *W ou le souvenir d'enfance,* and which also surface in his dreams as images of a suffering child: his sobs as he passes a concentration camp ward reserved for incurably ill children (17), the horror of the destruction of a deformed foetus-like infant (37), the tearful recognition that there will be no Christmas (100), tears over a tomb (103), and a sobbing child who has lost a ball (123).

While numerous scenes of fulfilled sexuality might suggest an absence of repression and therefore of symbol, psychoanalysts can find ample material to explore in a menacing and fascinating serpent (in a dream entitled "L'Œdipe-Express" —83), in five images of narrow passages (two of them associated with intestines), and in an actress's small breasts, which make him think of his mother (92). One other remarkable recurring motif of Perec's dreams is the presence of crowds who intrude into his private life. He repeatedly finds that he is sharing his apartment with strangers. When he eats, when he works, and when he makes love, he often finds himself surrounded by crowds.

Claude Mauriac[26] and Catherine David[27] note that Perec hides things from his reader. The names of his friends, his wife, his mistresses, are designated only by initials. In his introduction Perec explains an occasionally used symbol which represents a deliberate omission. The "authenticity" and potential for scientific analysis of the texts are further undermined by Perec's writing and rewriting of them, "ces rêves trop rêvés, trop relus, trop écrits" (Preface).

The most characteristic style of the narrations is a simple, almost neutral, occasionally telegraphic style, relying heavily on nouns and verbs:

> Une collègue de bureau, M., me rend visite. Survient G., une autre collègue; peut-être nous dérange-t-elle: en tout cas notre scène à trois provoque chez moi un grand déplaisir.

> Nous donnons plusieurs rendez-vous; nous nous retrouvons nombreux. Départ pour le défilé: perspective d'une grande fête. Problème d'un costume. (87)

The most self-consciously literary passage is the first, which relies on stylistic repetitions, self-analysis, and nouns in apposition to recreate the haunting image of a concentration camp:

> Comme de bien entendu, je rêve et je sais que je rêve comme de bien entendu que je suis dans un camp. Il ne s'agit pas vraiment d'un camp, c'est une image de camp, un rêve de camp, un camp-métaphore, un camp dont je sais qu'il n'est qu'une image familière, comme si je faisais inlassablement le même rêve, comme si je ne faisais jamais d'autre rêve, comme si je ne faisais jamais rien d'autre que de rêver de ce camp. (1)

A literary exercise, a sociological resource, and despite all, a treasure of analyzable symbols, Perec's *La Boutique obscure* is also a part of the unfinished autobiography. Distorted reflections of his everyday life, preserved images of his childhood terrors, fantasies based on his fears, joys, and preoccupations, all blurred by conscious and unconscious repressions and a literary concern for the text, these dreams constitute a partial portrait of Perec which complements the other traces of his passage.

• • •

Espèces d'espace:[28] a book about kinds of spaces which begins with "The page" obviously has a very particular orientation. As Claude-

Henri Roquet observes, "Il s'agit d'écrire l'espace, il s'agit d'espaces écrits et décrits, il s'agit, au fond, d'écriture."[29]

Responding in a very personal way to Lamartine's vain desire to drop an anchor amidst the flow of time, Perec seeks to fix in writing the imperturbable flow of space which eradicates traces of his passage:

> J'aimerais qu'il existe des lieux stables, immobiles, intangibles, intouchés et presque intouchables, immuables, enracinés; des lieux qui seraient des références, des points de départ, des sources. (122)

In the absence of a "pays natal," of a family estate with its familiar tree planted on the day of his birth, and an attic full of childhood memories, Perec is obliged to struggle against the erosion of past spaces and the memories attached to them. Since for him, "L'espace est un doute: il me faut sans cesse le marquer, le désigner; il n'est jamais à moi, il ne m'est jamais donné, il faut que j'en fasse la conquête" (122), Perec forms a meticulous, willfully banal project to describe and thereby preserve the fragile boundaries of space which frame his life:

> Ecrire, essayer méticuleusement de retenir quelque chose, de faire survivre quelque chose: arracher quelques bribes précises au vide qui se creuse, laisser, quelque part, un sillon, une trace, une marque ou quelques signes. (123)

The ultimate repository—and starting point—of the project is the blank page, the first vital space, which he hesitantly begins to fill, at first with nothing more than the repeated notation, "J'écris." Between this hesitant, painfully self-conscious beginning and the very personal conclusion, Perec describes spaces ranging from the smallest practical living space, the bed, to the vastness of the universe, stopping to consider along the way, room, apartment, building, street, neighborhood (*quartier*), city, countryside, country, continent, and world.

Despite the profound seriousness of Perec's purpose, to create a trace of his passage, the book is one of his most charming. Its tone is often humorous:

> Il y a plein de petits bouts d'espace... un... de taille plutôt modeste à l'origine, a atteint des dimensions assez colossales et est devenu Paris,

cependant qu'un espace voisin, pas forcément moins doué au départ, s'est contenté de rester Pontoise. (14)

There is also a refreshing charm in many of Perec's most banal observations, as he forces the reader to look at the obvious:

> Le lit est un des rares endroits où l'on se tienne dans une position grosso modo horizontale. Les autres sont d'un emploi beaucoup plus spécialisé: Table d'opération, banquette de sauna, chaise longue, divan de psychanalyste... (29)

> L'alignement parallèle de deux séries d'immeubles détermine ce que l'on appelle une rue: la rue est un espace bordé, généralement sur ses deux plus longs côtés, de maisons; la rue est ce qui sépare les maisons les unes des autres, et aussi ce qui permet d'aller d'une maison à l'autre, soit en longeant, soit en traversant la rue. (65)

> [Le quartier est] la portion de la ville dans laquelle on se déplace facilement à pied ou, pour dire la même chose sous la forme d'une lapalissade, la partie de la ville dans laquelle on n'a pas besoin de se rendre, puisque précisément on y est. (79)

Part of the charm of the book also resides in the use of several of Perec's favorite techniques: lists and catalogs (zero points, steps in the writing process, uses for a piece of paper, geographical terms, some 200 verbs associated with moving into a new apartment) and mathematical games (the height of a piece of paper, 1/1000 of a millimeter thick, when folded in half fifty-eight times, equals the distance from the Earth to the sun).

Perec's discussion of bedrooms is consciously placed under the sign of Marcel Proust. Following a vivid evocation of a bedroom in which he slept in Rock, Cornwall, during the summer of 1954, Perec observes:

> L'espace ressuscité de la chambre suffit à ranimer, à ramener, à raviver les souvenirs les plus fugaces, les plus anodins, comme les plus essentiels. La seule certitude coenesthésique de mon corps dans le lit, la seule certitude topographique du lit dans la chambre, réactive ma mémoire, lui donne une acuité, une précision qu'elle n'a presque jamais autrement. (33)

Perec's attempts to stabilize the ephemeral recollections of his past parallel Proust's search for lost time. He brings to the task a more meticulous, scientific approach (he is, after all, a social scientist by training): "C'est sans doute parce que l'espace de la chambre fonctionne chez moi comme une madeleine proustienne (sous l'invocation de qui tout ce projet est évidemment placé: il ne voudrait rien être d'autre que le strict développement des paragraphes 6 et 7 du premier chapitre de la première partie *(Combray)* du premier volume *(Du côté de chez Swann)* de A *la recherche du temps perdu*) que j'ai entrepris, depuis plusieurs années déjà, de faire l'inventaire, aussi exhaustif et précis que possible, de tous les *Lieux où j'ai dormi."* (34). He proposes a thematic organization of the 200 rooms in which he has slept, with classifications ranging from personal bedrooms, to train cars, to police stations and hospitals.

The book is designed to encourage and teach the reader to look differently at the familiar space around him or her. As part of his methodological exposition, he proposes a plan for the definition of a street, a plan which he places under the general quideline, "S'obliger à voir plus platement" (71). Perec himself applies the guideline to four projects, the first a 1975 article, "Tentative d'épuisement d'un lieu parisien,"[30] in whose introduction he explains his concern to record, "ce qui se passe quand il ne se passe rien, sinon du temps, des gens, des voitures et des nuages."[31]

In *Espèces d'espaces* he announces a twelve-year project to study the evolution of twelve places in Paris of personal interest to him, which he proposes to describe at the rate of two per month, yielding 288 texts, twenty-four devoted to each place. He never completed this project, but he did publish two others based on the same principle, one very modest, the other grandiose. The first is an article published in 1976 in *Nouvelles Littéraires,* "Notes concernant les objets qui sont sur ma table de travail," in which he inventories and describes a very limited space, his writing desk, and muses upon a larger project, the history of each object thereupon, "Ce sera, une fois encore, une manière de marquer mon espace."[32]

The grandiose project, announced and described in *Espèces d'espaces* is, of course, *La Vie mode d'emploi,* "J'imagine un immeuble parisien dont la façade a été enlevée..." (57). He explains the mathematical guidelines which will shape the narrative and identifies an important source, a drawing by Saul Steinberg entitled "The Art of Living," portraying an apartment building with twenty-three rooms visible, which contain an astonishing variety of things that Perec delights in listing (58-60).

Espèces d'espaces is Perec's most successful work of nonfiction. A city planner refers to it as "une bible pour les urbanistes."[33] It provides a delightful and original plan for looking at the world in new ways, in order to capture the essence of the spaces that surround us. Stylistically and thematically it relates to all of Perec's work from the first words of *Les Choses* (the decoration of an ideal apartment) to the last of *La Vie mode d'emploi* (Valène's unfinished painting of the apartment building). The obsessive presence of the concentration camp—evoked in a grotesque but authentic German memorandum of 1943 listing the types of plants needed to decorate the crematorium at Auschwitz—the many references to his own personal spaces, and the explicitly expressed desire to mark the traces of his passage, inscribe Perec's scientific pursuit of the spaces around us within the boundaries of his personal search for a stable past.

• • •

Early in 1978, Perec published *Je me souviens,*[34] a series of forty-eight numbered memories, most of them from the period 1945-1961, each beginning with the phrase, "Je me souviens." Some of the memories are no more than a list of evocative proper nouns:

> Je me souviens de la Baie des Cochons. (299)
> Je me souviens de Joseph Laniel. (337)
> Je me souviens du journal *Radar*. (356)
> Je me souviens de Mister Maggoo. (376)

Others are memories of "times when":

> Je me souviens quand les voitures pouvaient klaxonner, et des klaxons qui faisaient "rheuh-rheuh." (377)
> Je me souviens de l'époque où un immeuble (de dix étages) qui venait d'être achevé au bout de l'avenue de la Sœur-Rosalie était le plus haut de Paris et passait pour un gratte-ciel. (52)
> Je me souviens qu'après la guerre on ne trouvait presque pas de chocolat viennois, ni de chocolat liégeois, et que, pendant longtemps, je les ai confondus. (23)
> Je me souviens quand il y avait des petits autobus bleus à tarif unique. (111)

There are others that evoke slogans, word games, fashions, monuments, stars, and catastrophes.

The collection carries the subtitle, "Les Choses Communes I." In a *Le Monde* interview,[35] Perec describes three additional volumes of "Les Choses Communes" that he planned to write, and explains that the subtitle refers to the journal *Cause Commune* which he had founded with Jean Duvignaud and Paul Virilio as "une sorte de sociologie de la vie quotidienne."

In his description of *Je me souviens* published on the back cover, Perec again insists on the quotidian and common nature of the memories evoked in the volume: "des petits morceaux de quotidien, des choses que telle ou telle année, tous les gens d'un même âge ont vues, ont vécues, ont partagées." The details presented are willfully banal and offered without pretense to an audience whom Perec invites to continue his work by filling several blank pages at the end of the book with their memories.

The form of the memories and Perec's description of the project leave the impression that he is absent from the book. Monique Pétillon finds that "toute couleur personnelle est soigneusement gommée, neutralisée par une écriture qui se veut pure énonciation d'un air du temps impalpable et fané."[36] Chantal Labre calls Perec "l'anti-Proust,"[37] and Serge Koster, too, describes the book in terms which oppose Perec's self-effacing project to Proust's search for meaning and purpose in memories of the past: "Il ne s'agit pas d'une expédition à la recherche du temps perdu, ni d'un recours aux techniques de l'autobiographie; il s'agit de laisser remonter à la surface les éléments 'banals' qui tissent la trame quotidienne et collective d'une génération..."[38]

While Perec's memories are usually collective, they are also selective. It is sufficient to look through the carefully prepared index, noting thirty-nine references to movie actors, twenty-five references to film, eighteen references to movie theaters, twenty-six to *music-hall,* and sixteen references to language, to recognize that in the conscious or unconscious process of selection, Perec has imposed his own interests, tastes, and obsessions on these memories.

Some of the memories are personal and seem far removed from the search for universality suggested by Perec and his reviewers:

> Je me souviens que l'une des premières fois que je suis allé au théâtre ma cousine s'est trompée de salle—confondant l'Odéon et la Salle

Richelieu—et qu'au lieu d'une tragédie classique, j'ai vu *L'Inconnu d'Arras* d'Armand Salacrou. (31)
Je me souviens qu'à la fin de la guerre, mon cousin Henri et moi marquions l'avance des armées alliées avec des petits drapeaux portant le nom des généraux commandant des armées ou des corps d'armées... (37)
Je me souviens comme c'était agréable, à l'internat, d'être malade et d'aller à l'infirmerie. (64)
Je me souviens que je devins, sinon bon, du moins un peu moins nul en anglais, à partir du jour où je fus le seul de la classe à comprendre que *earthenware* voulait dire "poterie." (67)
Je me souviens que j'ai été très surpris d'apprendre que mon prénom voulait dire "travailleur de la terre." (150)
Je me souviens des mois de mai à Etampes quand on commençait à aller à la piscine. (321)
Je me souviens quand je me suis cassé le bras et que j'ai fait dédicacer le plâtre par toute la classe. (393)
Je me souviens du bain que je prenais le samedi après-midi en revenant du collège. (419)
Je me souviens quand j'allais chercher du lait dans un bidon de fer blanc tout cabossé. (435)

These and many more personal reflections are so many elements of a personal autobiography, presented as unrelated fragments (effect of "coupure") and intermingled with less personal memories.

Perec recognizes the existence of errors in his memories; "Lorsque j'évoque des souvenirs d'avant-guerre, ils se réfèrent pour moi à une époque appartenant au domaine du mythe; ceci explique qu'un souvenir puisse être 'objectivement' faux" (*post-scriptum*, p. 119). This tacit recognition of a "subjective" truth limits further the universality of these details. In the *post-scriptum* and in the *Le Monde* interview, Perec, almost gleefully, reveals his errors: "Le livre fourmille d'erreurs. Mais cela fait partie du flou. Il y a quelque chose d'incertain dans le petit tremblement du passé."[39]

As a result of this "petit tremblement," the errors which Perec embraces, the personal memories, and the style which Perec imposes upon them, *Je me souviens* is not the simple trivia game that it at first appears to be. Chantal Labre compares the book to *W ou le souvenir d'enfance* and finds in both works the same concern to anchor the present upon the past, " 'Tant que le souvenir n'existe pas,' la vie n'a pas d'assise... les lieux, les événements sont dénués de réalité."[40] In *W*, Perec confronts the fragmented images of his early childhood and attempts to understand and explain them by juxtaposing those fragments with the fictional narrative of Gaspard Winckler. In *Je me souviens*, Perec confronts the same fragmentation of his past and imposes upon the fragments concision and universality as he inserts his personal memories into a collective framework.

Je me souviens is an evocation of Perec's own past, in which others of the same generation will certainly recognize images of themselves. It is nonetheless a personal past, though a past without order or coherence. The memories are like images in a shattered mirror which reflects bits and pieces of a life, and which Perec holds out to himself and to us as a portrait containing all the details he is willing to reveal. Along with the incomplete autobiography of *W*, the personal reflections in *Espèces d'espaces*, and the obscure and even more fragmented scenes of *La Boutique obscure*, they form a partial autobiography. Perec, recognizing his ambivalent feelings as he begins his autobiography, writes in the opening pages of *W*: "une fois de plus, les pièges de l'écriture se mirent en place. Une fois de plus, je fus comme un enfant qui joue à cache-cache et qui ne sait pas ce qu'il craint ou désire le plus: rester caché, être découvert."[41] In his four autobiographical works, Perec leaves fragmented traces of his passage which partially reveal and partially obscure his past.

4

POETRY, THEATER, AND FILM

Alphabets • *La Clôture et autres poèmes* • *L'Augmentation* • *La poche
Parmentier* • *Un homme qui dort* • "Récits d'Ellis Island" • "Série Noire"

PEREC'S PUBLISHED VERSE APPEARED IN JOURNALS AND LIMITED
editions and in two collections, *Alphabets*,[1] and *La Clôture et autres
poèmes*.[2]

Perec composed the 176 poems of *Alphabets* between January 1974
and May 1976. They were generated by an almost unimaginable constraint
which Perec explains on the volume's back cover:

> Chacun des cent soixante-treize textes de ce recueil est un onzain, un
> poème de onze vers, dont chaque vers a onze lettres. Chaque vers utilise
> une même série de lettres différentes, quelque chose comme une gamme,
> dont les permutations produiront le poème selon un principe analogue à
> celui de la musique sérielle: on ne peut répéter une lettre avant d'avoir
> épuisé la série. Tous les poèmes ont en commun les dix lettres les plus
> fréquentes de l'alphabet français: E, S, A, R, T, I, N, U, L, O. La
> onzième lettre est l'une des seize restants: B, C, D, F, G, H, J, K, M,
> P, Q, V, W, X, Y, Z. Il y a onze poèmes en B, onze poèmes en C,
> etc..., soit au total onze alphabets complets, c'est-à-dire 16 x 11 = cent
> soixante-seize poèmes.

Each "heterogrammatic" poem is presented in two typographical forms,
once as an 11 x 11 grid, demonstrating its conformity to the constraint, and
then as free verse, using more or less standard French syntax.

The first poem in the volume, a "B" poem, that is, one whose added
letter in each line is B, uses relatively clear imagery and syntax:

Satin, or bleu, trouble sain.   SATINORBLEU
Rite: nous balbutions la réalité.   TROUBLESAIN
Nous brûlons.   RITENOUSBAL
                                                        BUTIONSLARE
Abrite la brune toison, brutalise   ALITENOUSBR
le bâton suri, ablutions errantes: ULONSABRITE
oubli...   LABRUNETOIS
                                                        ONBRUTALISE
                                                        LEBATONSURI
                                                        ABLUTIONSER
                                                        RANTESOUBLI

The constraint forces on this poem, as on nearly all of them, an elliptic, almost telegraphic, style. The economy of expression by no means implies, however, a poverty of expression. In these poems as in other works of Perec written within constraints, the limits he imposes force him to find rare and surprising words and images.

In this respect, the first poem is not really typical. With the exception of the past participle "suri" (meaning "soured"), the vocabulary, like the syntax, is fairly simple. The conciseness of expression may at first bewilder the reader, but one quickly perceives that the poem narrates a sexual encounter in four stages:

1) Desire: A vision of the woman dressed in gold and blue satin arouses the poet's desire (trouble sain).

2) Courtship: The couple engages in the traditional mating ritual (rite) in which the reality—that they are experiencing sexual desire ("Nous brûlons")—is hidden beneath intentionally imprecise language ("Nous balbutions la réalité).

3) Intercourse: The concise style caricaturizes the male and female attitudes; the female contains ("abrite la brune toison") and the male ("bâton suri") brutalizes. The efforts of the couple are "ablutions errantes."

4) Ecstasy: "oubli."

The ritualistic nature of the encounter, suggested by the words "rite" and "ablutions," is accentuated by the simplified syntax the form imposes. The result is comic. Mating is caricaturized as the speeded-up, trivialized accomplishment of a biological and social ceremony in which the male attacks the willing female, and they both experience pleasure and release.

Most of the poems in the collection are less clear. One of the inescapable results of Perec's project is that the volume must include, not

Count beggunning letters [handwritten annotation]

just one short poem with eleven K's, but eleven poems with eleven K's. And eleven poems with eleven W's! The problems that this must have posed for Perec are unimaginable. The resulting poems, amazing and ingenious as they are, also present problems for the reader. The most successful of the W and K poems are those in which Perec's wit comes to his rescue, as in Poem 141, which carries the title "Western":

> Wairn loue Stewart.
> —Il nous suit l'or à New Town!
> Le saurien Louis Warton tua Sir Lewis,
> alentour.

> Wars! [circled with handwritten marking]

> Winetou l'outlaw serine un slow traînart, Wise Lou...

In another W poem (131) whose theme is New Orleans jazz, English again provides many words. And one of the Y poems (171) is completely in English (but no clearer for that).

One certain effect of the constraint placed on the poems in the volume is an unequaled musicality. Since each line contains exactly the same letters (and in most cases then the same sounds), there is a harmonic repetitiveness of sounds from beginning to end of each poem (and between poems) which makes them a pleasure to recite and hear. Robin Buss, reviewing the collection in the *London Times,* notes, "The most successful poems in the collection are those which carry the insistent music of their eleven letter scale but emerge magically from the straitjacket of the form."[3]

The themes of the poems are remarkably varied, but one which recurs consistently is art. The second poem in the collection, which is the subject of an article by Mireille Ribière,[4] quotes Mallarmé and seems to refer specifically to the art of *Alphabets:*

> Aboli, un très art nul ose,
> bibelot sûr, inanité (l'ours-babil:
> un raté...) sonore
>> Saut libérant s'il boute
>> l'abus noir ou le brisant
>> trublion à sens:
>>> Art ébloui!

The interrupted phrase "aboli...bibelot...inanité...sonore" refers to Mallarmé's sonnet, "Ses pus ongles," but there are also references to two other poems by Mallarmé: "Un coup de dé" and "Le cantique de St. Jean." The first word of Perec's poem, "aboli," echoes the use of the verb in "Un coup de dé" and the obsessive need to eliminate chance. Perec, committed to making art obey laws of necessity, continues the Mallarméan venture, despite the obvious perils: the first stanza introduces positive expressions of artistic mastery ("très art," "ose," "sûr," "sonore") interrupted by negative pitfalls ("aboli," "nul," "inanité," "babil," "raté"). The Mallarméan phrase, "inanité sonore," summarizes the positive and negative elements which surround Perec's attempt to eliminate chance.

The uncertainty of the first stanza gives way in the second to the "saut libérant," which accompanies the artistic mastery of imposed constraints, the paradoxical burst of creative freedom. The form and imagery of the stanza are similar to those of Mallarmé's "Cantique," in which the severed head of the martyred saint surges upwards with the repressed energy of years of constraint. The final exclamation represents the dazzling triumph of form.

Occasionally Perec finds his self-imposed form not quite constraining enough, and he adds additional difficulties as in Poem 108:

Pulsation
éruption
saler la prison
tu es au point
le ras où prit lent aloi pur
se nier

(stop)

nul
à ôter l'an
puis nature
si pôle
sort nu
pire uni là

(stop)

The grid reveals the additional imposed constraints:

PULSATIONER	PULSATIONER
UPTIONSALER	UP
LAPRISONTUE	L P
SAUPOINTLER	S　P
ASOUPRITLEN	A　　P
TALOIPURSEN	T　　P
IERSTOPNULA	I　　　P
OTERLANPUIS	O　　　P
NATURESIPOL	N　　　P
ESORTNULAPI	E　　　P
REUNILASTOP	R　　　　P

The letters of the first line are the same as the first letters of each line; and the added letter, P, moves one space at a time from the first letter in line one to the last letter of line eleven. The resulting poem (whose telegraphic syntax is accentuated by the word "stop" at the end of each stanza) seems to be about eroticism, perhaps auto-eroticism.

Two other poems deserve to be cited as examples of Perec's mastery of an impossible medium. Poem 100 describes an evening sky:

Opalines rutilantes
pourpres au lointain
les pourtours platinés
perlant ou irisant le pouls

éruption

autre laps inopiné où l'astre pâli sort nu

The lights and colors evoked in the first four lines give way to the eruption of the sun's last rays, and then, after a delay, a pale star (the moon?) appears.

Poem 103 is less clear in meaning, but in its vagueness there is a Verlainien suggestion of sadness amidst a heavy air of fatigue and a feeble glimmer of hope:

Rose nuptiale, unis la torpeur
à ton pli soupesant l'ironie.

Pars-tu? La nuit s'éplore loin.

Ta surprise n'a tu l'opéra
si l'on put puiser—ô, l'antan tu—
l'espoir.

First published in 1976 in a limited edition, and later republished
with several other poems, the heterogrammatic poems of *La Clôture* were
generated by a process similar to that of *Alphabets*. The series of available
letters includes the eleven most common (E, S, A, R, T, I, N, U, L, O, C)
plus one additional free letter per line. The free letter permits Perec more
latitude and the resulting poems are richer. According to Harry Mathews,
they are largely autobiographical.[5] In the eleventh poem, the images of
claustration and death echo the major themes of the collection:

Clôture.
Sa fin.
Nul écrit
Sa mort n'a souci.
L'expulsion trace sa ligne,
court sur toi, clandestine.

L'arc-bouter au sol pince,
au flot inscrit sur le bon cadastre

où linceul naît corps.

The first stanza recreates the sensation of death closing in and then leaving
no trace (Perec's mother?), but the focus of the poem is on the other, "toi,"
the witness or living victim of the death, who is shut off, banished by the
indifferent process which tears apart two people. The notion of "clôture" is
here, as elsewhere in the collection, both a process and a result, related to
the notion of "coupure" as evoked in *W ou le souvenir d'enfance,* a
separation, a termination, an isolation.

The second stanza represents a reaction, an attempt to reverse the
process, to hold onto the other, to hold onto life as suggested by images of

earth, water, and the land (registry). But the efforts are vain; death—the shroud—is already inscribed in the birth process.

The volume includes along with the seventeen poems of *La Clôture,* another extended heterogrammatic poem called "Ulcérations," first published separately in 1974, and in which every line uses only the letters of the word "ulcérations"; "Métaux," a collection of seven heterogrammatic "sonnets" (14 lines of 14 letters); some incidental poems based on constraints; and a curious collection, "Trompe l'œil," which includes six poems in which every word exists in both English and French. For example:

```
ICY
MIRE  VENUE
N OSE
ENGRAVER
BRIBES  PLATES
D UNE
AVERSE  SALE  (p. 32)
```

La Clôture also includes a poem simply entitled, "Un poème" (p. 83), one of two poems published by Perec which were written freely with no formal constraint; the other freely written poem, "L'Eternité," was published originally by Orange Export Ltd,[6] just months before Perec's death:

L'Eternité

Venue de l'imperceptible
convexité de l'œil
—ce par quoi on sait que la terre est ronde—
l'éternité est circulaire
mais plate

le coussin est (montagne) érosion
le tapis pénéplaine

il n'y a plus de déchirure
dans l'espace ni dans moi

: le monde avant qu'il ne se
plisse, une ondulation d'herbes
entre l'est et l'ouest

une ligne imaginaire va parcourir
ce balancement oblique

on sait que les eaux
s'y partageraient s'il y avait
de l'eau

mais il y a seulement
cette soif de pliure

des silhouettes se superposent

le long de cette arête fictive
immobiles dans leur mouvement

chaque instant est persistence et mémoire

l'horizon dans son absence
est une hésitation émoussée

la préfiguration tremblante
du *corral*
où se tapit sa catastrophe.

Eternity appears as a rounded surface, different and desirable because of its wholeness: "il n'y a plus de déchirure dans l'espace ni dans moi." Its curved space surrounds smoothly, womb-like, without edges or breaks. Relief is the result of an ancient, gentle erosion, which creates a carpet-like softness, making cushions of mountains.

This image of a world without edges carries nonetheless on its surface a "soif de pliure." It seems to call forth the image of the real world which is cut by "une ligne imaginaire," "cette arête fictive," "l'horizon dans son absence." Eternity is a lost garden, "une ondulation d'herbes," whose gentle contours enfold, but whose loss is already prefigured upon the enclosing circular space by the latent cutting lines ready to emerge in the form of the catastrophic corral.

In an interview with Jean-Marie Le Sidaner, Perec addresses the role of constraint in his poetry:[7]

Je n'envisage pas pour l'instant d'écrire de poésie autrement qu'en m'imposant de telles contraintes.... L'intense difficulté que pose ce genre de production, et la patience qu'il faut pour parvenir à aligner, par example, onze "vers" de onze lettres chacun ne me semble rien comparées à la terreur que serait pour moi d'écrire "de la poésie" librement.

It would be fascinating to explore this terror, for it seems to lie at the heart of Perec's creativity. The "free" poems are clearer and consequently more revealing; is it the dread of revealing himself freely which forces Perec to hide behind the screen of constrained syntax and replace sincere emotion with word play? Or is it merely that his imagination needs the inspiration of constraints and that the absence of inspiration gives rise to the terror of the blank page?

At any rate, the poems written with constraints, ingenious and musical though they may be, appear to the reader as little more than brilliant exercises and do not generally invite the thorough exegesis which their originality merits.[8]

• • •

Perec's theater includes three plays in German,[9] five short texts in French, three of which were set to music,[10] and two major works published together in *Théâtre I:*[11] *L'Augmentation,* and *La Poche Parmentier.*

L'Augmentation, first performed at the Théâtre de la Gaïté-Montparnasse on February 26, 1970, was inspired by Perec's fascination with organizational flowcharts; it expresses the thought processes and actions of an employee who asks his superior for a salary increase. Each of the employee's initiatives is broken down into logical components as might be fed through a computer and is expressed by one of six characters:

Les six comédiens représentent la machine, mais l'efficacité de la machine est de formuler en les décomposant toutes les pensées qui se mêlent dans la tête d'un homme: ici, d'un homme qui va demander une augmentation... A partir de l'organigramme, c'est la démarche d'une pensée humaine que j'ai voulu démonter.[12]

The title, which at its most banal level means a salary increase, is also a type of puzzle which grows increasingly complex at each stage, and a figure of rhetoric (*incrementum*) "qui consiste à empiler des séries d'arguments pour emporter la conviction" (back cover).

The six main characters symbolize different possible elements of a thought. The play consists of their formulations, presented to the audience, which follows the progress of the employee, who is never seen and is called "vous." The audience thereby participates in the thought process and in the adventure. For example, the first thought is simply to go and ask the supervisor for a raise. The six different characters and their expressions relative to the thought are as follows:

1) La proposition: Vous allez voir votre Chef de Service pour lui demander une augmentation.
2) L'alternative: Ou bien votre Chef de Service est dans son bureau, ou bien votre Chef de Service n'est pas dans son bureau.
3) L'hypothèse positive: Si votre Chef de Service était dans son bureau, vous frapperiez et vous attendriez sa réponse.
4) L'hypothèse négative: Si votre Chef de Service n'était pas dans son bureau, vous guetteriez son retour dans le couloir.
5) Le choix: Supposons que votre Chef de Service ne soit pas dans son bureau.
6) La conclusion: En ce cas vous guettez son retour dans le couloir. (11)

The presence and role of the fifth character, the choice, suggest that the thought process in which the characters are engaged is as much creative as narrative. At each step, as in a "choose your own adventure" book, the playwright, through character number five, creates the next step in the chain of creative thought.

The adventure that character number five chooses to create for the audience is, not surprisingly, convoluted. The supervisor is not in on several occasions, or he is too busy to talk to the employee. The employee therefore waits in the hall, chats with the secretary, walks through the offices, and makes appointments to see his supervisor. Months pass; on the first two occasions when the employee finally gains an audience, he is interrupted by the arrival of a new, seventh, character, "The Measles," first the supervisor's, then the employee's. After several refusals and the compensatory awarding of a prestigious medal, the employee finally wins the promise that his request will be passed on. Six more months pass with no raise, the employee again decides to speak to his supervisor, and the play ends as the process is about to recommence.

Although most of the hypotheses and choices are predictable (with the obvious exception of the intervention of "The Measles"), the play has the potential to entertain audiences, for the inherent tedium of the series of propositions is broken by several comic effects: comically pretentious speeches, irony, cruel humor, melodramatic exaggerations, choral repetitions, and elliptically shortened propositions.

Nonetheless, the play as first performed had little success. Bertrand Poirot-Delpech reviews it politely in *Le Monde*,[13] but concludes, "Même réduit à moins d'une heure, l'exercice se ressent de ne reposer que sur un seul effet répété sans cesse."

La Poche Parmentier, first presented at the Théâtre de Nice on February 12, 1974, borrows situations, themes, and even dialogue from the repertory of contemporary theater, specifically from the plays of Sartre, Camus, Ionesco, and Beckett; but the characters find a unique solution to the problem of existence as posed by these playwrights.[14]

The nameless characters, an old woman, a man, a woman, a young man, a young girl, and a servant, are locked in a room which has no apparent exit. They try to remember or invent past crimes which might explain their presence there. The only door which they can find opens onto a stairway which leads down to an interior courtyard where a guard is posted. (There are suggestions that this Sartrian hell is really no more sinister than an insane asylum.)

Within this oppressive setting, some of the characters express a Beckettian cheerfulness. Despite the cynical pessimism of the others, the young girl, the man, and the old woman wait and hope, looking for and inventing when necessary positive signs of the possibility of escape, or at least of an eventual improvement in their situation:

Jeune Fille: Il suffit de faire un tout petit pas en avant chaque jour.
Femme: Un pas en avant et deux en arrière, vous voulez dire! Ça s'appelle marcher à reculons!
Jeune Homme: On tourne en rond...
Femme: En tout cas, on piétine!
Homme: C'est toujours comme cela, au début... On ne sait pas très bien où l'on va...
Jeune Fille: C'est peut-être une question de méthode. (71)

La Vieille Femme: Je sais bien, ça ne va pas vite, mais quand même,
tous les jours, on progresse un petit peu. (77)

La Vieille Femme: Vous avez raison, oui, je suis sûre qu'on finira par
s'en sortir! Ça ne peut quand même pas durer comme ça cent
sept ans! (77)

For an undetermined length of time they have confronted the absurdity of their situation by peeling potatoes, piles and piles of them, which litter the set. This seemingly absurd response, which recalls Ionesco's plays of the late fifties and early sixties (there are four specific borrowings from *La Cantatrice Chauve*), becomes more than a meaningless, mechanical escape. For the characters find beauty, meaning, and purpose in the humble potato:

C'est du solide, la pomme de terre, on peut toucher, ça existe, c'est pas
comme vos trucs à la noix! C'est pas du vent! Ça s'épluche, ça se
lave, ça se laisse cuire, ça se mange en purée, en salade, en rondelles!...
De tout temps les Arts ont glorifié la pomme de terre! Le tryptique de
Lucas de Bintje, le retable de Karl-Philippe-Emmanuel Cartoufle, dit
Cartolfini, Le Nain, le buste de Parmentier par Houdon, Meissonnier,
L'Angélus de Millet! Vincent Van Gogh! (68)

The potato is not only an abundant, inexpensive, and nourishing food, it is also a plant with a history and a hero. The characters take turns narrating the history of the potato from antiquity to the present, emphasizing particularly the role of Antoine Parmentier, who in the eighteenth century encouraged the production and consumption of potatoes in France. It is a story that the characters have told over and over again, and whose enthusiastic retelling leads them into a frantic song and dance.

The potato saves the characters from despair not only because it keeps them physically and mentally occupied, but especially because of the story to tell. For telling stories seems to represent a form of salvation. They tell and invent their own personal stories and amuse themselves with other authentic, borrowed, or imagined tales: the story of the man who hid from the Germans during the war; the story of the wonderful garden; the story of the walled-up bat; the story of the man who returns to the village of his childhood; the story of the young woman whose honor is saved, the story of the seasons; and, of course, the story of the potato.

They discover in the course of their storytelling that they have an additional resource; as actors on a stage (there are several self-consciously clever winks at the audience), they can perform as well as narrate their stories. They act out the "Model Family," and the drama of the man who tries to lure an architect into marrying his daughter. Ultimately play-acting provides a denouement, albeit an artificial one: the characters decide to act out the final scene of *Hamlet*. And at the end of *La Poche Parmentier,* as at the end of *Hamlet,* the stage is littered with the corpses of the players.

The play had little chance of charming an audience in Nice. (One thinks of the American première of *Waiting for Godot* staged in Miami.) Michel Cournot, reviewing the production in *Le Monde*[15] manifests his disappointment and that of the audience: "Le public est clairsemé et manifeste une hostilité sourde."

• • •

Perec created or participated in the creation of nine films[16] ranging from the literary and biographical "Flaubert" to the commercial and popular "Série Noire."

His first film was the cinematic adaptation of *Un Homme qui dort,* directed by Perec and Bernard Queysanne and produced by Pierre Neurisse and Hamdi Essid in 1974. Filmed in black and white, and using limited resources, "Un Homme qui dort" employs two actors and the streets of Paris to recreate the intellectual and psychological adventure of the young protagonist. A female voice recites the text as the camera follows the student's mechanical, indifferent, and occasionally purposeful wanderings from his room through the streets of Paris. The film was not commercially successful but received encouraging critical praise; Mireille Amiel writes in *Cinéma 74:*[17] "Il importe peu ensuite d'en voir les quelques insuffisances (La modicité des moyens économiques n'y est pas étrangère), ce premier film est un film exemplaire, calme, à l'écart des modes et conscient, contemporain d'elles, à l'abri des facilités, exempt à jamais des démagogies, orgueilleux mais proche d'une souterraine fraternité." Georges Franju in *Positif*[18] calls it "un film... que je tiens pour une exceptionnelle réussite de cinéma onirique."

Récits d'Ellis Island

"Vous vous souvenez de votre passage à Ellis Island?"
"Qu'est-ce qui vous est arrivé à Ellis Island?"
"Est-ce que ce lieu vous rappelle quelque chose?"
"Vous avez des souvenirs d'Ellis Island?"
"Est-ce que ce lieu vous rappelle quelque chose?"
"Et vous êtes arrivé à Ellis Island... Comment c'était?"

These questions, monotonously repeated to the American immigrants whom Perec interviews in his 1980 documentary film "Récits d'Ellis Island,"[19] reveal his obsessive fascination with the details of American immigration, and with the island as a symbol of that process.

Perec first visited Ellis Island in 1978 with filmmaker Robert Bober, drawn to it for reasons that he did not clearly understand at the time. In the film's prologue, we watch Perec thumbing through a scrapbook of Ellis Island photos as his voice-over narration announces his purpose in terms of two questions:

A Paris quand nous disions que nous allions faire un film sur Ellis Island, presque tout le monde nous demandait de quoi il s'agissait. A New York, presque tout le monde nous demandait pourquoi. Non pas pourquoi un film à propos d'Ellis Island, mais pourquoi nous. En quoi cela nous concernait-il, nous Robert Bober et Georges Perec?

Il serait sans doute un peu artificiel de dire que nous avons réalisé ce film à seule fin de comprendre pourquoi nous avions le désir ou le besoin de le faire. Il faudra bien, pourtant, que les images et les textes qui vont suivre rendent compte, non seulement de ce que fut Ellis Island, mais du chemin qui nous y a conduits.

In response to the first question, What is Ellis Island?, Perec provides a partial answer with a litany of facts, beginning with a summary of the island's history from the time of the Dutch colony, including its purchase by Samuel Ellis, the transfer of its ownership from the Ellis family to the Berry family to the State of New York and finally to the federal government, which on January 1, 1892, opened the immigration center on the island. There follows an abundance of facts and figures including a breakdown of the national origins of the 16 million immigrants who passed through the immigration center from 1892 to 1954, the names of the ports from which they sailed, and the names of the boats they took. Bober's camera continues the narration, movingly capturing the ruins (as filmed in 1978) and vandalized remains of the once-imposing structure.

An old film clip, still pictures, and the words of a U.S. Park Service guide complete the answer to Perec's first question. The guide, dressed in a ranger's uniform and hat, takes a group of mostly American tourists through the island's principal structure, followed closely by Bober's camera. The reality of the Ellis Island experience unfolds through the guide's subtitled words, as he describes the hours and occasionally days on the island which awaited each of the 16 million immigrants, and tells the humorous anecdotes which constitute the folklore of Ellis Island.

The guide's attitude ranges from bemusement to concern, a grave concern transmitted to the tourists and through Bober's camera to the film audience. For the story of Ellis Island is not always a pretty one. Paradoxically for the millions who had come seeking freedom and opportunity—and that purpose resounds emphatically in the interviews which constitute an important appendix to the film—the United States Immigration Service was obliged to establish a dehumanizing series of controls to process the immigrants who numbered as many as 10,000 a day. Their purpose was to register, but also, increasingly through the years, to limit. Immigrants with certain diseases, mental deficiencies, political tendencies, or insufficient resources were denied permission to enter the United States. In the history of the island, only 2 percent of the immigrants were denied admission, but that represents nonetheless 250,000 individual and often family tragedies. Between 1892 and 1954 there were 3,000 suicides on Ellis Island.

As the camera and microphone register the guide's evocation of the Ellis Island experience, two details emerge: the large main hall was originally divided by metal barriers into "cattle runs" (in the words of the guide), which were not eliminated until 1911; and immigration authorities made use of a system of letters to mark certain immigrants:

> dans la légende du Golem, il est raconté qu'il suffit d'écrire un mot, Emeth, sur le front de la statue d'argile pour qu'elle s'anime et vous obéisse, et d'en effacer une lettre, la première, pour qu'elle retombe en poussière

> sur Ellis Island aussi, le destin avait la figure d'un alphabet. Des officiers de santé examinaient rapidement les arrivants et traçaient à la

craie sur les épaules de ceux qu'ils estimaient suspects une lettre qui
désignait la maladie ou l'infirmité qu'ils pensaient avoir décélée:

C,   la tuberculose
E,   les yeux
F,   le visage
H,   le cœur
K,   la hernie
L,   la claudication
SC, le cuir chevelu
TC, le trachome
X,   la débilité mentale

les individus marqués étaient soumis à des examens beaucoup plus
minutieux. Ils étaient retenus sur l'île plusieurs heures, plusieurs
jours, ou plusieurs semaines de plus, et parfois refoulés. (35)

Perec's personal obsession with the fate of European Jews during
the Nazi occupation makes him particularly sensitive to the "herding" and
labeling procedures described as part of the Ellis Island ritual. His editing
of the text and film emphasizes, perhaps exaggerates, this disquieting
underside of America's welcome to the immigrants of the world. It is
clearly not Perec's intent to expose American freedom as an unreliable
myth. His fear of and fascination with manifestations of fascism—a fear
and a fascination which mark in many forms his fiction as well as his
autobiographical works—draw him, perhaps unconsciously, towards these
images of cattle runs and the branding of immigrants.

A historical phenomenon, a symbol of hope, an "Island of Tears,"
an insensitive, dehumanizing system—all of these elements form a
composite reality which eloquently answers Perec's first question. To the
question, What does it represent to you?, Perec first responds by trying to
understand what it represented for the original immigrants:

c'était la Golden Door, la Porte d'or
c'était là, tout près, presque à portée de la main,
l'Amérique mille fois rêvée,
la terre de liberté où tous les hommes étaient égaux,
le pays où chacun aurait enfin sa chance,
le monde neuf, le monde libre où une vie nouvelle
allait pouvoir recommencer

> Mais ce n'était pas encore l'Amérique:
> seulement un prolongement du bateau,
> un débris de la vieille Europe
> où rien encore n'était acquis,
> où ceux qui étaient partis
> n'étaient pas encore arrivés,
> où ceux qui avaient tout quitté
> n'avaient encore rien obtenu (34)

The image of a doorway which separates the past from the future, a doorway which temporarily imprisons those who had left but who had not yet arrived, is an important key to Ellis Island's fascination for Perec. This small island which is no longer Europe but which is not yet America is, as Perec will say later, a nowhere land, inhabited by people cut off from their past.

Perec continues his exploration of the meaning of Ellis Island by trying to imagine what it must represent for the others, the American tourists with whom he visits the island, who are for the most part descendants of Ellis Island immigrants:

> ce n'est pas pour apprendre quelque chose qu'ils sont venus,
> mais pour retrouver quelque chose,
> partager quelque chose qui leur appartient en propre,
> une trace ineffable de leur histoire
> quelque chose qui fait partie de leur mémoire commune
> et qui a façonné au plus profond la conscience qu'ils ont d'être
> américains. (36)

One recognizes in this search for a "trace ineffable de leur histoire" Perec's own personal obsession with traces of his lost past. The first scene of "Récits d'Ellis Island" showing Perec leafing through an old scrapbook of Ellis Island photographs, which appears at first glance to be a writer's natural interest in primary source material, suddenly leaps out at the enlightened viewer, transformed into Mallarmé's Hamlet, "lisant au livre de lui-même." Photos of Perec himself stare back from the album. The image had already appeared in *W ou le souvenir d'enfance,* in which the narrator seeks traces of his past in "Photos jaunies... témoignages rares... et documents dérisoires" (22). The discontinuity of his past and of his memories of it leads Perec, almost without his knowing why, to Ellis Island, where he mingles among the American tourists who there seek tangible traces of their past. Knowing, however, that this particular place can provide no trace of his own past, Perec identifies with the very absence of trace:

> Ellis Island est pour moi le lieu même de l'exil,
> c'est-à-dire le lieu de l'abence de lieu, le non-lieu, le nulle part.
> C'est en ce sens que ces images me concernent, me fascinent, m'impliquent,
> comme si la recherche de mon identité passait par l'appropriation de ce lieu-dépôtoir où des fonctionnaires harassés baptisaient des Américains à la pelle.
> ce qui pour moi se trouve ici
> ce ne sont en rien des repères, des racines ou des traces,
> mais le contraire: quelque chose d'informe, à la limite du dicible,
> quelque chose que je peux nommer clôture, ou scission, ou coupure,
> et qui est pour moi très intimement et très confusément lié au fait même d'être juif (42)

What Perec finds is not a trace of his past, but the confirmation of the absence of traces, its opposite in fact, which he vaguely identifies with the notions of "clôture, ou scission, ou coupure." This is one of the few texts in which Perec confronts what it means, to him, to be Jewish. His traumatic separation from his mother, the break which interrupts an otherwise happy childhood, is, in a sense, his own personal variation on the pattern of Jewish life. It is a pattern which thousands of Ellis Island immigrants have recreated as their passage from immigrant to American cuts them off from their past.

In "Récits d'Ellis Island" Perec generalizes on his own experience in terms which relate his life to the history of his people and to the experiences of all immigrants forced to flee their homelands:

> j'aurais pu naître, comme des cousins proches ou lointains, à Haïfa, à Baltimore, à Vancouver
> j'aurais pu être argentin, australien, anglais ou suédois
> mais dans l'évantail à peu près illimité de ces possibles,
> une seule chose m'était précisément interdite:
> celle de naître dans le pays de mes ancêtres,
> à Lubartow ou à Varsovie.
> et d'y grandir dans la continuité d'une tradition,
> d'une langue, d'une communauté.

Quelque part, je suis étranger par rapport à quelque chose de moi-même;
quelque part, je suis "différent", mais non pas
différent des autres, différent des "miens": je
ne parle pas la langue que mes parents parlèrent,
je ne partage aucun des souvenirs qu'ils purent avoir,
quelque chose qui était à eux, qui faisait qu'ils
étaient eux, leur histoire, leur culture, leur espoir, ne m'a pas été
transmis. (44)

An essential element of his life: continuity, wholeness, tradition, is missing.
He finds Ellis Island an apt symbol of that lack and therefore seeks to
discover on the island, in the stories of those who passed through there, and
in the emotions of the American descendants of Ellis Island immigrants who
tour the island with him, a resonant kinship, not a tangible document, not
even a memory, but rather a spiritual trace of his own suspended life.

"Vous vous souvenez de votre passage à Ellis Island?"
"Qu'est-ce qui vous est arrivé à Ellis Island?"
"Est-ce que ce lieu vous rappelle quelque chose?"
"Vous avez des souvenirs d'Ellis Island?"
"Est-ce que ce lieu vous rappelle quelque chose?"
"Et vous êtes arrivé à Ellis Island... Comment c'était?"

These questions which Perec repeats obsessively to the subjects he
interviews in the film draw few meaningful responses. Ironically, one finds
that Perec's Ellis Island experience is more profound, more emotional, than
that of the real Ellis Island immigrants. For them, it is a distant memory,
effaced by their absorption into American life. Their accounts pass quickly
over Ellis Island and dwell on their successes and failures adapting to the
American life-style which they were in fact creating. They do not share
Perec's sense of something severed, something lost.

"Récits d'Ellis Island" is a powerful documentary about a unique
historical and sociological phenomenon. But it is also a surrogate autobiography. The place which is not a place, but rather a doorway, responds
to the deep yearning within Perec to open the sealed doorways which shut
him off from his own past. Perec looks for and finds images of his lost
past, a reflection, a trace of himself, in the photos of Ellis Island
immigrants, in the stones and debris of the island, and in the memories of
those who passed through there.

• • •

"Série Noire"[20] is Perec's most successful film, in fact the only one which brought him into contact with a major studio (Gaumont) and a large popular audience. In collaboration with the film's director, Alain Corneau, Perec adapted for the screen the Jim Thompson novel, *A Hell of a Woman*.[21] He is credited as coauthor of the scenario and author of the dialogues.

The film follows the sordid misadventures of Frank Poupart, brilliantly interpreted by Patrick Dewaere, as he evolves from a likeable, smooth-talking bathrobe salesman and petty thief to a pathetic, deranged murderer. The plot is well constructed and dramatically paced.

Poupart's first murder owes as much to Dostoyevsky as to Jim Thompson; he kills and robs an unpleasant, miserly old woman who had been exploiting her simple-minded niece. But in the same scene, Poupart and the plot turn ugly as he kills his friend Tikides in order to establish for the police a likely explanation of the crime: Tikides appears to be an intruder shot to death by his dying victim.

The charming bathrobe salesman follows the murder of his best friend with the murder of his wife who had begun to suspect him of the first crime. Poupart pathetically hands over the profit of his crime to his blackmailing employer, and the film ends as, penniless, he prepares to run off with the beautiful, simple-minded niece of the murdered old woman, chanting hopefully, "On n'a plus rien à craindre."

The dialogue, mostly mumbled or shouted, is full of the vulgar slang which traditionally characterizes films and books of the "série noire" (the film's title is the generic term for sordid gangster films and novels with a high content of sex and violence—from the name of a publisher specializing in the genre).

Perec's involvement in this commercial film (moderately popular in theaters, it has been featured on prime time television and is readily available on video cassette) is certainly atypical. Although his vision is often nightmarish and preoccupied with the failure of human aspirations, his treatment of sordid subjects is usually tempered with humor or games, or by intellectual and esthetic considerations. Despite the skillful construction of the plot and invention of dialogue, and despite remarkable performances, "Série Noire" remains an unattractive and fundamentally uninteresting portrait of criminal psychopathology.

5

LA VIE MODE D'EMPLOI

THE SUCCESS OF PERCIVAL BARTLEBOOTH'S PUZZLEMAKING PROJECT, which from beginning to end of *La Vie mode d'emploi*[1] holds together the hundreds of stories that constitute the history of the apartment building at 11, rue Simon-Crubellier, depends initially on the creation of a special glue, which will permit him to glue together the pieces of the finished puzzles:

> Bartlebooth chercha un procédé qui lui permettrait... de récupérer les marines initiales; pour cela il fallait d'abord recoller les morceaux de bois, trouver un moyen de faire disparaître toutes les traces de coups de scie et redonner au papier sa texture première. (42)

The search for the ideal glue leads Bartlebooth through his accomplices Smautf and Morellet to Kusser, a scientist at the Ecole Polytechnique, Morellet's boss, and reportedly a distant descendant of the German composer Johann Sigismund Kusser (or Cousser). We learn a great deal more about the German composer than we do about the gluemaker who gives his formula to Morellet, who, as a result of his efforts, will be supported for the rest of his life in near idleness. Gluemaker Kusser is never mentioned again; like his glue, and like the watercolors his glue helps to reconstitute, he disappears without leaving a trace.

For the watercolors, the puzzles and the glue are part of a mechanism whose *raison d'être* is to leave no trace. The watercolors, after having been glued to a plywood backing, cut into 750-piece puzzles, and put back together according to a rigorous schedule, were to be separated from their backing and transported back to the spot where they had been painted, to be dipped into a detersive solution, "d'où ne ressortirait qu'une feuille de papier Whatman intacte et vierge. Aucune trace, ainsi, ne resterait de cette opération qui aurait pendant cinquante ans, entièrement mobilisé son auteur" (158). The esthetic and philosophic principle upon which Bartlebooth founds his life's activity requires this self-negating circularity: "inutile, sa gratuité étant l'unique garantie de sa rigueur, sa perfection serait circulaire: une succession d'événements qui, en s'enchaînant, s'annulerait: parti de rien, Bartlebooth reviendrait au rien, à travers des transformations précises d'objets finis" (157).

This precise transformation of finite objects through a fifty-year process depends on mathematical and engineering specifications and the will to apply them. The guidelines were established by Bartlebooth as a young man in his early twenties seeking an orderly course of activities to occupy his idleness:

1) For ten years, from 1925 to 1935, he would learn the art of watercolor.

2) For twenty years, from 1935 to 1955, he would travel the world, stopping every two weeks in a new port to paint a picture of it. He would paint 500 watercolors, each with the same format (65 cm x 50 cm) and send them when completed back to Paris to be made into puzzles of 750 pieces.

3) For twenty years, from 1955 to 1975, he would put the puzzles back together, one every two weeks, and have them glued, separated, and dissolved.

These are the broad outlines of the project whose execution, especially in the second phase, requires careful attention. Five years before their departure in 1935, Smautf began to prepare, studying visa regulations, opening bank accounts, reserving hotels, and booking passages. The description of the four trunks which accompany Bartlebooth (427-29) reveals the meticulousness of Bartlebooth's planning; their contents, organization, and arrangement seem to foresee every eventuality. And while the twenty-year itinerary was not completely mapped out in advance, allowing Bartlebooth the flexibility to choose his course as he traveled, the schedule of activities in each port followed a routine which permitted travel, study, sketches, and painting to be accomplished efficiently in the allotted fortnight.

Organization, schedules, precise calculations, and meticulous preparation—all seem to suggest that Bartlebooth possesses a maniacal sense of order and purpose. Yet he does not foresee all, order all, calculate all. In an uncharacteristically sardonic tone, the novel invites us to consider the faults of Bartlebooth's system. The narrator questions his decision to paint 500 watercolors, when it would have been more precise to do 480 (two per month) or 520 (one every two weeks). The roundness of the figure imposes an inexactness on the time allotted to each painting. The vagaries of travel and shipping eventually imposed other irregularities as did occasional delays in the reconstruction of a puzzle. But the narrator dismisses these minor irregularities which are obscured by the ultimate failure of the project:

> Si l'on peut parler d'un échec global, ce n'est pas à cause de ces petits décalages, mais parce que, réellement, concrètement, Bartlebooth ne parvint pas à mener à terme sa tentative en respectant les règles qu'il s'était donné (sic): il voulait que le projet se referme sur lui-même sans laisser de traces, comme une mer d'huile qui se referme sur un homme qui se noie, il voulait que rien n'en subsiste, qu'il n'en sorte rien que le vide, la blancheur immaculée du rien, la perfection gratuite de l'inutile, mais s'il peignait cinq cents marines en vingt ans, et si toutes ces marines furent découpées par Gaspard Winckler en puzzles de sept cent cinquante pièces chacun, tous les puzzles ne furent pas reconstitués, et tous les puzzles reconstitués ne furent pas détruits à l'endroit même où, à peu près vingt ans plus tôt, les aquarelles avaient été peintes. (481-82)

Bartlebooth's will to complete his self-destructive project, his need to leave no trace, to drown himself and his project beneath the smooth surface of an oil-covered sea, is frustrated by two accidents: his blindness and his death. But even without these accidents, could the project have succeeded? Is the gratuitous perfection envisioned by Bartlebooth, the empty, traceless perfection, compatible with the human spirit? Certainly not in the universe created by Georges Perec, a universe obsessed with traces. Even in the midst of his search for artistic perfection and his attempts to master impossible constraints, Perec tolerates glitches, intentionally disrupts the systems he creates, leaving tell-tale traces, the "clinamen," which is an essential trace of the artist's presence.[2]

Bartlebooth's project carried within itself the seeds of its own failure. The meaninglessness of the puzzles' reconstitution seems to affect increasingly his vigor and efficiency:

Au début, il allait vite, il travaillait avec plaisir, ressuscitant avec une
sorte de ferveur les paysages qu'il avait peints vingt ans auparavant....
Puis, au fil des années, c'était comme si les puzzles se compliquaient de
plus en plus... (167)

Gaspard Winckler's skills as a puzzlemaker had advanced faster than
Bartlebooth's skill as a puzzlesolver, and it becomes increasingly difficult
for him to finish the puzzles in the prescribed period. At the same time,
Bartlebooth begins to experience a disorientation with respect to the object
of the exercise; while his companion Smautf can still find in the
reconstitution of the paintings meaningful resonances of their travels,

Pour Bartlebooth, ils n'étaient plus que les pions biscornus d'un jeu
sans fin dont il avait fini par oublier les règles, ne sachant même plus
contre qui il jouait, quelle était la mise, quel était l'enjeu, petits bouts
de bois dont les découpes capricieuses devenaient objets de cauchemars,
seules matières d'un ressassement solitaire et bougon, composantes
inertes, ineptes et sans pitié d'une quête sans objet. Majunga, ce n'était
ni une ville, ni un port, ce n'était pas un ciel lourd, une bande de
lagune, un horizon hérissé de hangars et de cimenteries, c'était
seulement sept cent cinquante imperceptibles variations sur le gris,
bribes incompréhensibles d'une énigme sans fond, seules images d'un
vide qu'aucune mémoire, aucune attente ne viendrait jamais combler,
seuls supports de ses illusions piégées. (167)

The endlessness, the repetitiveness, but especially the senselessness
of the reconstitution of the puzzles gradually takes its toll on Bartlebooth.
Their pitiless transformations of colorful scenes from an adventurous life
into bits and pieces of a solitary game, the images of those geographical
spaces which he had visited and painted and which symbolize twenty years
of his life, fragmented, cut up into meaningless shreds of color, overwhelm
him. His "illusions piégées," his belief not only in his capacity to complete
the fifty-year project, but also in its purpose and value, are doubly
sabotaged, on one hand by the skill of the puzzlemaker and Bartlebooth's
mortality, but more surely by the illusory nature of the purpose and value of
a project based on gratuitous emptiness.

The novel ends with a summary of the activities of the apartment
building at the moment of Bartlebooth's death, punctuated by the haunting
variation of the phrase, "C'est le vingt-trois juin, mille neuf cent soixante-

quinze et il est presque huit heures du soir" (599). At that precise moment, "Assis devant son puzzle, Bartlebooth vient de mourir. Sur le drap de la table, quelque part dans le ciel crépusculaire du quatre cent trente-neuvième puzzle, le trou noir de la seule pièce non encore posée dessine la silhouette presque parfaite d'un X. Mais la pièce que le mort tient entre ses doigts a la forme, depuis longtemps prévisible dans son ironie même, d'un W" (600).

The "W" is the signature of the puzzlemaker, Gaspard Winckler, whose victory over Bartlebooth, "la longue vengeance qu'il a si patiemment, si minutieusement ourdie" (22), represents the triumph of gamesmanship with all its components: ruse, mystery, strategy, enigma, and play, over the empty meaninglessness of the Bartlebooth project. From 1935 to 1955 Winckler had created 500 individual puzzles, but he had also invented inter-puzzular games of cat and mouse which stymy and baffle Bartlebooth, eventually prolonging the project and preventing its completion.

The three-and-one-half-page "préambule" to the novel (15-18), analyzing the art of the puzzle, is reinserted into the novel as an introduction to the description of Winckler's role as puzzlemaker (248-51). The passage refutes the commonly held belief that the picture determines the degree of difficulty of a puzzle. While this may be true for mass-produced cardboard puzzles, all cut from the same pattern, it is certainly not true of the artistic puzzle whose cut is a carefully studied calculation based on the design and on the personality of the puzzlesolver:

> L'art du puzzle commence avec les puzzles de bois découpés à la main lorsque celui qui les fabrique entreprend de se poser toutes les questions que le joueur devra résoudre, lorsque, au lieu de laisser le hasard brouiller les pistes, il entend lui substituer la ruse, le piège, l'illusion: d'une façon préméditée, tous les éléments figurant sur l'image à reconstruire... serviront de départ à une information trompeuse. On en déduira quelque chose qui est sans doute l'ultime vérité du puzzle: en dépit des apparences, ce n'est pas un jeu solitaire: chaque geste que fait le poseur de puzzle, le faiseur de puzzle l'a fait avant lui. (250)

The novel tells us little about the artist puzzlemaker Gaspard Winckler. He was born in 1910 in La Ferté-Milon, on the Canal de l'Ourcq, and learned woodworking from a M. Gouttman.[3] In Winckler's living room is a fascinating wooden chest which he had sculpted "in his youth" depicting in amazing detail scenes from Jules Verne's *L'Ile*

Mystérieuse. In 1932, at the age of 22, he responded to Bartlebooth's published announcement inviting candidates to submit samples of their skill as puzzlemakers. Winckler's entry, "La Dernière Expédition à la Recherche de Franklin," made from a painting by his wife, delighted Bartlebooth, who hired Winckler for the project.

Winckler spent two years purchasing equipment and setting up his workshop. Early in 1935 the paintings started arriving, one approximately every two weeks. Each painting was attached with a specially prepared glue to a plywood board, studied exhaustively for several days, then cut, polished, and taken to be stored in a vault at the Société Générale.

Marguerite Winckler died in November 1943 in childbirth. For five or six months, Winckler was immobilized by grief, after which he removed from the apartment everything that reminded him of her and returned to his workshop and the eleven watercolors waiting to be made into puzzles.

After 1955, when he had finished his 500 puzzles, he spent his time making toys, rings, and "miroirs de sorceries,"[4] reading newspapers, and playing *jacquet* with Morellet; the ordinarily calm and taciturn Winckler became on occasion surprisingly violent in the midst of their daily card games.

It is no accident that Perec's puzzlemaker hero is named Gaspard Winckler. It is the name which Perec previously gave to two of his alter-egos in *W ou le souvenir d'enfance*. *La Vie mode d'emploi* is full of artists, four of whom (Valène, Hutting, Marguerite Winckler, and, of course, Bartlebooth) assume major importance. But the real artist-hero of the novel is the triumphant puzzlemaker Gaspard Winckler.

In several interviews, Perec acknowledges the role of the puzzlemaker and the importance of the puzzle in the novel:[5]

> Tous mes propres sentiments sont dans le livre tout entier, ils ne sont pas dans un personnage particulier. Il y en a un toutefois que j'aime plus que les autres, Winckler, l'artisan qui fabrique les puzzles.... C'est l'artisan, c'est-à-dire qu'il est un peu comme moi. C'est lui qui fabrique les puzzles, comme moi je fabriquais le livre.[6]

> C'est un livre avec lequel on joue, je crois, comme on joue avec un puzzle.[7]

> A la limite mon rêve serait que les lecteurs jouent avec le livre... qu'ils voient comment tous les personnnages s'accrochent les uns aux autres

et se rapportent tous, d'une manière ou d'une autre, à Bartlebooth, comment tout cela circule, comment se construit le puzzle.[8]

Au centre de ces histoires bâties comme des puzzles, l'aventure de Bartlebooth tiendrait évidemment une place essentielle.[9]

L'image du puzzle est pour moi une image fondamentale pour expliquer la construction de ce livre.[10]

Perec makes no secret of *some* of the rules governing the construction of his puzzle/novel. In the article "Quatre Figures pour *La Vie mode d'emploi*," he illustrates the principle which guides the narrative through the 99 spaces/chapters of the building/novel—"la polygraphie du cavalier"[11]—and its relationship with the novel's division into six parts (and incidentally explains why there are 99 instead of 100 chapters—the little girl biting off one corner of a square "biscuit Lu"); he also explains the "bi-carré latin orthogonal d'ordre 10" which provided a matrix for distributing twenty-one times two series of ten elements (a total of 420 elements) throughout the novel, establishing for each chapter a unique list of forty-two elements which the chapter incorporates. In the *Magazine Littéraire* interview, he elaborates the nature and function of these generating elements:

Au départ, j'avais 420 éléments, distribués par groupes de dix: des noms de couleur, des nombres de personnes par pièce, des événements comme l'Amérique avant Christophe Colomb, l'Asie dans l'Antiquité ou le Moyen Age en Angleterre, des détails de mobilier, des citations littéraires, etc... J'avais, pour ainsi dire, un cahier des charges: dans chaque chapitre devaient rentrer certains de ces éléments. Ça c'était ma cuisine, un échaffaudage que j'ai mis près de deux ans à monter, et qui ne me servait que de pompe à imagination.[12]

Perec provides more specific information about the generating elements of two chapters. In "Quatre Figures...," he publishes a page from his notebook listing the forty-two elements to be included in chapter 23; among them are Verne, Joyce, *agendas, boiseries, Moyen Orient, bibliothèque, bas/chaussettes, Moby Dick, parallèlipipède, cuivre/étain, pendules/horloge*. In a March 1977 interview on his work in progress, he talks about the elements for chapter 43:

En consultant mes grilles, je peux vous dire que le chapitre 43, qui n'est pas encore écrit, se déroulera au cinquième étage à droite. Il y aura dans ce chapitre quelqu'un debout, se servant d'un plan; il y aura une citation de Proust et une de Joyce; il y aura au minimum deux personnes, peut-être plus, dont l'une sera un fournisseur (mais ce peut être un tableau, un mercier avec une dame achetant une bobine de fil).[13]

Perec has provided keys to three other puzzles which he includes in his novel:

1) Pages 102-06 contain the precise descriptions from a sales catalog published by the Moreau Tool Co. of twenty-two home repair kits. "Ce catalogue, je l'ai composé comme un poème. Il a ses strophes, ses retours de mots: vanadium, métal chromé, son refrain, 'Garantie totale un an, garantie totale un an' "[14]

2) Pages 292-98 comprise a "compendium" of the novel, 179 succinct summaries of events which the painter Serge Valène enumerates. Perec's German translator, Eugen Helmlé, reveals the constraints imposed by Perec on these 179 lines: "Il y avait donc plusieurs contraintes à respecter: le résumé succinct d'une des aventures relatées dans le livre, la limitation des 60 frappes par ligne, et la lettre qui se déplaçait du dernier caractère de la première ligne au premier caractère de la soixantième ligne."[15] (In the first sixty lines, the letter A moves one space at a time from the end to the beginning; in the next sixty lines, it is the letter M, and in the final fifty-nine lines it is E.)

3) Perec in *Atlas de Littérature Potentielle*[16] reveals the names of Oulipo members hidden in the descriptions of twenty-four portraits by painter Franz Hutting (352-54). Three examples:

3) Septième Sévère apprend que les négotiations avec le *Bey n'about*iront que s'il lui donne sa sœur Septimia Octavilla (Bénabou).

19) L'acteur Archibald Moon hésite pour son prochain spectacle entre Joseph d'*Arimathie ou* Zarathrousta (Harry Mathews).

21) Le docteur LaJoie est radié de l'ordre des médecins pour avoir déclaré en public que William Randolph Hearst sortant d'une projection de Citizen *Kane aurait mon*nayé l'assassinat d'Orson Welles (Raymond Queneau).

In many of his public declarations about the novel, Perec invites the reader to play with it, to try to find other puzzles which he has hidden. Readers have responded, some with great ingenuity. Ewa Pawlikowska writes:

> Le nom écrit et dit de Perec (soit Pérec) est doublement évoqué dans le Compendium du chapitre LI de *La Vie mode d'emploi:* d'abord il y figure en anagramme *percé,* dans le vers 73: "l'Ancêtre du docteur croyant avoir percé l'énigme du diamant," dont les chiffres 7 et 3 nous cachent la date de naissance de Perec, un 7 mars. Le chapitre 73 (LXXIII) est, ensuite, en lui-même d'une importance capitale dans la structure du roman. Il contient "Histoire du bourrelier" Albert Massy mais aussi celle du fameux cycliste Lino Margay dont "le bois de la piste lui a arraché toute la moitié droite du visage." C'est un des personnages les plus mutilés de *La Vie mode d'emploi....* Cette histoire, écrite sous l'enseigne du roi-mage, révèle la mutilation et le manque qui constituent en eux-mêmes une métaphore de l'écriture née d'un vide bio-graphique.[17]

Bernard Magné, in an article entitled "Noms naufragés,"[18] provides a close reading of chapter 40. By juxtaposing passages from that chapter with other published and nonpublished texts by Perec, he demonstrates brilliantly the obsessive presence of certain letters, syllables, words, and themes, which associate the apparently unrelated events of the chapter with Perec's loss of his parents as narrated in *W ou le souvenir d'enfance.*

There is still much to be uncovered in the novel. Among the "Pièces Annexes" of the novel is a "Post-scriptum" in which Perec lists the thirty authors whom he cites in the course of the novel. Bernard Magné has explored Perec's strategies in incorporating these literary borrowings into the novel.[19] Among the authors cited is Perec himself, and the careful reader can easily locate allusions to and quotes from his other works as well as extended passages adapted from *Un Homme qui dort* and from *L'Augmentation.*

Perec suggests that we read his novel twice, "d'abord d'affilée puisqu'il y a cette histoire de Bartlebooth qui court d'un bout à l'autre. Ensuite en se servant de l'index pour reconstituer la trajectoire des personnages."[20] He offers as an example the story of Mlle Crespi.[21] Following, with the aid of Perec's index, the story of another very minor character, Geneviève Foulerot, the reader encounters an accumulation of fascinating and enigmatic details.

The first time the reader encounters Geneviève, she is naked, walking to the bathroom with an egg in her hand to take a bath and wash her hair (36). The novel refers on several occasions to Geneviève's bath. A photo pinned to her door shows her, "vêtue d'un maillot de bain deux-pièces... à côté d'une piscine démontable" (246). The photo is from a catalog for which Geneviève, an actress and model, posed. Other photos of her in the catalog portray her, "à bord d'un canoë de studio avec un gilet de sauvetage" and "revêtue d'un peignoir de bain." Geneviève's baby sleeps in "un moïse en jonc tressé blanc" (246).

On the wall of Geneviève's apartment is a strange painting done by her grandfather, inspired by a detective novel called *L'Assassinat des poissons rouges*.[22] Some of the objects included in the painting are:

> un bocal de poissons
> un pot de résédas
> un ciel arrondi comme un dôme
> un lac
> une table d'école avec un trou pour l'encrier
> une carafe d'eau
> un de ces verres appelés flûtes
> un chandelier dont le socle est un admirable œuf d'ivoire
> un paysage de bord de mer
> une crique bouillonnante
> une barque
> un grand miroir
> un jarre de pickles
> un biberon géant (283-84)

The explanation of the painting offered by the summary of the novel *L'Assassinat des poissons rouges* adds that the events take place near a city called Valdrade, that the inspector's name is Waldémar, that one of the suspects is named Jarrier, and that the daughter of another suspect drowned herself to preserve her honor. Two sentences in the explanation of the circumstances of the crime bring together strikingly several of these obsessive elements of liquids and containers:

Il vit que les poissons rouges manquaient d'eau et vida la carafe d'eau
dans le bocal que Jarrier avait volontairement renversé en arrivant.
(289)
Il a négligeamment versé dans la carafe d'eau le contenu d'un petit
flacon de fibrotoxine caché dans la tétine de son biberon géant. (288)

Geneviève Foulerot's personal story is touching, though incomplete. An aspiring actress, she left her parents' home in order to be able to keep and raise her fatherless baby. Her grandfather, an interior decorator and painter, is the only member of the family who is kind to her. She leaves her baby with the concierge every morning and picks him up in the evening after coming home and taking her bath.

The pieces of the "Geneviève puzzle" suggest a solution which includes the biblical story of Moses, who as a baby was set adrift in a bed made of reeds ("un moïse") and later rescued and adopted by a bathing princess. The story has obvious personal resonances for Perec, whose separation from his mother is metaphorically suggested in *W ou le souvenir d'enfance* by the possibility that young Gaspard Winckler was abandoned at sea by his mother.

• • •

While Gaspard Winckler represents Georges Perec the puzzlemaker, Serge Valène represents Perec as visionary storyteller. It is Valène who imagines the painting of the apartment building and its occupants as they are at 8 P.M. on June 23, 1975, which is the basis for the novel's descriptions.[23] In an article in *L'Education,* Perec confides, "Ceux qui iront chercher dans ma bibliographie verront que quand j'étais militaire, j'ai écrit, sous le nom de Serge Valène, un article dans *Les Lettres Nouvelles.* Ce peintre qui fait le tableau, c'est moi qui suis en train d'écrire le livre."[24]

Valène is old. His first appearance in the novel is as "le vieux peintre Valène" (38). He has lived in the apartment building for fifty-five years and has a unique perspective of the changes in the building over the years, "la vie de l'immeuble." Especially aware of changes brought about by the arrivals and departures of tenants, whose comings and goings are marked by moving vans, plumbers and electricians, cartons, stacks of furniture and fixtures, and sometimes police or undertakers, Valène is sensitive to the poetry of the building, the evocative power of its sounds and smells:

Les escaliers pour lui, c'était, à chaque étage, un souvenir, une émotion, quelque chose de suranné et d'impalpable, quelque chose qui palpitait quelque part, à la flamme vacillante de sa mémoire: un geste, un parfum, un bruit, un miroitement, une jeune femme qui chantait des airs d'opéra en s'accompagnant au piano, un cliquettement malhabile de machine à écrire, une odeur tenace de crésyl, une clameur, un brouhaha, un froufroutement de soies et de fourrures, un miaulement plaintif derrière une porte, des coups frappés contre des cloisons, des tangos ressassés sur des phonographes chuintants ou, au sixième droite, le ronflement obstiné de la scie sauteuse de Gaspard Winckler auquel trois étages plus bas, au troisième gauche, ne continuait à répondre qu'un insupportable silence. (91)

Valène seeks to create order out of the sights, sounds, smells, and emotions of the building, these bits and pieces of life which tend to disperse across the space of the building and through the fifty-five years of his familiarity with it. He will bring his memory and artistic vision to the grandiose project designed to freeze and create harmony of these fragments of life, the painting of the building which generates the narration. The obsessive presence of Bartlebooth's project, which spans nearly all of Valène's memories and helps to unite them, creates the cross-temporal vision at the end of the passage, Winckler's twenty years of noisy puzzlemaking, followed by Bartlebooth's twenty years of painfully silent solving.

His sense of the building as a living, growing organism leads him to imagine the building's demise, in a brutal cataclysmic destruction (281-82) or as a more natural process whereby the building is razed to make way for a park, a highway, or a new residential shopping complex (171-72). A long hallucinatory passage describes Valène's vision of the building's understructure:

Au-delà du premier niveau des caves auraient commencé les masses immergées: des escaliers aux marches sonores qui descendraient en tournant sur eux-mêmes, de longs corridors carrelés avec des globes lumineux protégés par des treillis métalliques et des portes de fer marquées de têtes de mort et d'inscriptions au pochoir, des monte-charges aux parois rivetées, des bouches d'aération équipées d'hélices énormes et immobiles, des tuyaux d'incendies en toile métallisé, gros comme des troncs d'arbres, branchés sur des vannes jaunes d'un mètre de diamètre, des puits cylindriques creusés à même le roc, des galeries bétonnées percées de place en place de lucarnes en verre dépoli, des réduits, des soutes, des casemates, des salles de coffres équipées de portes blindées. (444)

The hardness of gleaming rock and metal confer upon Valène's images of the first stage of the building's substructure a solidity and impenetrability which separate the living "human" apartment building above ground from the inhuman world below of mines, docks, garbage heaps, military installations, telephone switchboards, and computer terminals. His hellish vision penetrates deeper, past "des halètements de machines," "des locomotives à vapeur tirant des trucks," "des docks grouillants de passerelles," to a murky underground world of foul, muddy caverns inhabited by demonic, mythological monsters:

un monde de cavernes aux parois couvertes de suie, un monde de cloaques et de bourbiers, un monde de larves et de bêtes avec des êtres sans yeux traînant des carcasses d'animaux, et des monstres démoniaques à corps d'oiseau, de porc ou de poisson, et des cadavres séchés, squelettes revêtus d'une peau jaunâtre, figés dans une pose de vivants, et des forges peuplées de Cyclopes hébétés, vêtus de tabliers de cuir noir, leur œil unique protégé par un verre bleu serti dans du métal, martelant de leurs masses d'airain des boucliers étincelants. (447)

We have little information about Serge Valène's personal story. Perec gives us some dates: October 1919, he moves into the building; 1925, he begins giving Bartlebooth his watercolor lessons; August 1975, he dies. We also have a brief account of a sentimental adventure, his love for Marguerite Winckler, wife of the puzzlemaker. His dreams of running off with her were interrupted by her sudden death in 1943.

Although his personal story is undeveloped—for example, we don't know the names of any of his finished paintings—Valène marks the novel more directly than any other character. From the opening "oui" of the first chapter (perhaps a resonant continuation of Molly Bloom's monologue) to the death of Bartlebooth in the last, it is Valène's vision and affirmation of the poetic life of the building which create the novel. It little matters that he dies two months after Bartlebooth, leaving, like Balzac's Frenhoffer, a nearly blank canvas. His painting, in fact, contains only an outline of the building, empty and unoccupied; but that is enough, for his vision, captured by his alter-ego's words, which bring them to life within the reader's imagination, fills the canvas with the hundreds of characters and their belongings contained by the building throughout the years, fills the almost blank canvas with remembered stories.

For it is not the puzzles and games that make *La Vie mode d'emploi* a fascinating and memorable masterpiece. Nor is it the adventure of Bartlebooth, which holds the novel together. It is the stories, 107 of which are summarized by their titles on pages 691-94 of the "Pièces Annexes," and all of which come to life, triumphantly, painfully, comically, or tragically, in the 600 pages of the novel.

Consider the story of Maximilien and Berthe Danglars (former occupants of Bartlebooth's 3ème gauche), an important magistrate and his respectable wife who discover, quite by accident, that "le fait de dérober en public un objet de grande valeur déclenchait chez l'un et l'autre une sorte d'ivresse libidinale qui devint très vite leur raison de vivre" (491). For six pages the reader follows avidly the discreetly narrated account of their life of sex and crime, followed by their eventual arrest. The formerly elegant Mme Danglars appears at the end of the story, "assise sur un banc, rue de la Folie-Régnault, c'était une clocharde édentée, vêtue d'une robe de chambre caca d'oie, poussant une voiture d'enfant pleine de hardes diverses, et répondant au sobriquet de la Baronne" (495).

Only slightly less dramatic—and more mysterious—is the reversal of fortune of a physics teacher, Paul Hébert (5ème droite). In 1955 the beautiful Laetizia Grifalconi (4ème gauche) leaves her husband and two children to join Paul who had been transferred to Mazamet. Fifteen years later, "le jeune Riri," a former student of Paul, now stationed at Bar-le-Duc, sees his former teacher "habillé en paysan normand avec une blouse bleue, un foulard rouge à carreaux et une casquette [qui] proposait aux passants des charcuteries régionales, du cidre bouché, des gâteaux bretons, du pain cuit au four à bois.... Lorsque Paul Hébert lui rendit sa monnaie, leurs regards se croisèrent une fraction de seconde, et le jeune Riri comprit que l'autre s'était senti reconnu, et qu'il le suppliait de partir" (165).

There are also, of course, stories of acquired fortunes: the story of the reluctantly entrepreneurial Mme Moreau, or the unlikely "Histoire du bourrelier, de sa sœur et de son beau-frère:" a cyclist, Lino Margay, led at too fast a pace by his trainer Massy (the *bourrelier*), has a terrible accident which leaves his face grotesquely disfigured. Ravaged by guilt, Massy gives Margay his sister in marriage. Despite her good intentions, she cannot stand to live with her physically monstrous though loving husband.

Margay becomes involved in a small drug deal in Buenos Aires and is arrested and sentenced to three years in prison. While in prison, he discovers that his phenomenal memory permits him to retain all the details of the lives, records, and talents of the criminals with whom he is in contact, making him an invaluable human file of information on South American gangsters. He becomes a trusted counselor for the underworld, amasses a fortune which enables him to have his face surgically restored, reclaims his wife—whom he had never stopped loving—and lives happily ever after with her on Lake Geneva near Coppet (434-43).

It takes 600 pages to tell all of the stories in *La Vie mode d'emploi*. Here are brief summaries of a few others: the elaborate confidence game in which a surprisingly willing pharmacist is bilked of $1 million, which he was willing to spend for the vase used by Joseph of Arimathea to collect the blood of Christ (116-30); the career of Cinoc—for whose name Perec proposes twenty different pronunciations—who during fifty years as a "tueur de mots" eliminated thousands of "useless" words from the French language (360-66); the theft and plagiary of Dr. Dinteville's monumental edition of *De structura renum* by an unscrupulous colleague (575-81); Cyrille Altamount's touching letter to his wife explaining his relationship with her (539-44); the Marvel House Project for a chain of worldwide resorts (517-27). All of these stories, as well as dozens of others, are novels unto themselves. Each is animated by a remarkable passion. And even though many of the characters fail in their pursuits, even though Bartlebooth dies without finishing all his puzzles, even though Valène does not paint his painting, we are left with a tremendous sensation that the novel does demonstrate life and how to use it. Perec reflects on this sensation in the *Le Monde* interview:

> Ce mode d'emploi que vous proposez ironiquement de la vie en fait une chose plutôt noire. On part de rien, pour arriver à rien, après avoir fait beaucoup de choses inutiles.
>
> Oui, mais avec passion. Ce qui lie tous mes personnages entre eux, c'est la formidable passion qu'ils mettent à aller au bout du monde, à trafiquer des coquillages, à devenir acteur, à concevoir comme Valène cet immense tableau de l'immeuble.
>
> A quoi s'ajoute votre passion à vous pour écrire ce livre.

C'est pourquoi je crois qu'il y a en lui quelque chose qui relève du bonheur.[25]

Valène's unfinished painting of the apartment building is a nearly blank canvas: "Quelques traits au fusain, soigneusement tracés, la divisaient en carrés réguliers, esquisse d'un plan en coupe d'un immeuble" (602). All that exists is the square space of the canvas divided into smaller squares. On the opposite page of the book is Perec's schematic drawing of the building, a large rectangle, divided into smaller, labeled, squares and rectangles.

Both Perec's sketch and Valène's canvas are two-dimensional reproductions of the partitioned space of a Parisian apartment building, whose walls, ceilings, and floors, which appear as straight, carefully drawn lines, are human boundaries, rigorously defended frontiers that separate human lives. The distance between Cinoc's apartment and Dinteville's office can be measured in centimeters, the thickness of an apartment wall. Yet the two spaces, from a human perspective, are totally distinct: each contains different furnishings, arranged according to different tastes, different occupants, of course, with different longings, different passions, different stories.

The lines which in Valène's painting and Perec's drawing divide the building's living space represent an essential yet totally arbitrary reality: the boundaries of human lives. Both Perec and Valène acknowledge those boundaries, begin their work with them in mind, but both strive to remove them, to reconstitute as an artistic whole the fragmented space and life of the building. Alain Goulet describes Valène as "une pensée effervescente qui relie ce qui est disjoint, conserve la trace de ce qui a disparu."[26]

Kusser's glue is a plausible metaphor for the art of Valène and Perec.[27] Designed to leave no trace of the cuts in Bartlebooth's watercolors, it denies in a sense the work of the demonic Winckler, who during twenty years cut the scenes of Bartlebooth's travels into artistic but resistant fragments which frustrate Bartlebooth's attempts to restore the unity of his painted visions of the world.

Perec's novel is about life, about the lives of hundreds of characters; it is also about puzzles and the people who make and solve them; and finally it is about artists and their art. What the characters and the puzzles have in common is a complex dispersive evolution through time and space, to which the artist, the writer, and the puzzlesolver bring their confluent efforts to capture a permanent trace.

6

THE LAST WORKS

Un Cabinet d'amateur • "Le Voyage d'hiver"

GEORGE PEREC'S LAST NOVEL, *UN CABINET D'AMATEUR*,[1] PUBLISHED in 1979, represents an effort to climb out from under the shadow of his 1978 masterwork, *La Vie mode d'emploi.* In a June 1981 interview, Perec refers to the obsessive weight of *La Vie:* "J'ai du mal à m'en sortir. C'est d'ailleurs la raison pour laquelle je n'ai pratiquement rien écrit depuis deux ans." Addressing directly the relationship between his last two novels, he adds, "J'ai écrit *Un Cabinet d'amateur,* récit que j'ai publié après *La Vie mode d'emploi.* C'est un tableau qui représente une collection de tableaux et chaque tableau est une allusion à un chapitre du livre."[2]

The painting is Heinrich Kürz's "Un Cabinet d'amateur," which in the tradition of the German *Kunstkammer* portrays an art collector, Hermann Raffke, surrounded by his masterpieces. Each of the individual paintings portrayed has its unique subject, anecdote, and history, its own story. "Un Cabinet d'amateur" also has its story. In Perec's novel, all of these stories interact and through a complex system of references and reflections create a dazzling fiction and an original vision of the birth and death of art. Kürz included two of his own paintings among the dozens copied in "Un Cabinet d'amateur," one whose title is borrowed from Raymond Roussel:[3]

> La deuxième œuvre n'existe pas, ou plutôt elle n'existe que sous la forme d'un petit rectangle de deux centimètres de long sur un centimètre de large, dans lequel, en s'aidant d'une forte loupe, on parvient à distinguer une trentaine d'hommes et de femmes se précipitant du haut

d'un ponton dans les eaux noirâtres d'un lac cependant que sur les berges
des foules armées de torches courent en tous sens. Si Heinrich Kürz,
qui, confia-t-il un jour à Nowak, n'avait appris à peindre que pour faire
un jour ce tableau, n'avait pas décidé de renoncer à la peinture, l'œuvre
se serait appelé *Les ensorcelés du lac Ontario* et se serait inspirée d'un
fait-divers survenu à Rochester en 1891 (Gustave Reid en tira en 1907
un roman qui connut un certain succès): dans la nuit du 13 au 14
novembre, une secte de fanatiques iconoclastes fondée six mois plus tôt
par un employé de la Western Union, un tueur de bœufs et un agent
d'assurances maritimes, entreprit de saccager systématiquement les
usines, dépôts et magasins d'Eastman-Kodak. Près de quatre mille
boîtiers, cinq mille plaques, et quatre-vingt-cinq kilomètres de pellicule
de nitrocellulose furent détruits avant que les autorités puissent
intervenir. Pourchassés par la moitié de la ville, les sectaires se jetèrent
à l'eau plutôt que de se rendre. Parmi les soixante-dix-huit victimes
figurait le père d'Heinrich Kürz. (75-76)

Because Kürz abandoned painting, "Les ensorcelés du lac Ontario"
exists only as a tiny, 2- x 1-centimeter copy of a never realized painting. Its
details are visible only under a powerful magnifying glass. The novel
offers many examples of Kürz's skill at miniature reproduction and thereby
prepares us to accept thirty men and women (presumbably distinguishable),
a torch-bearing crowd, a pontoon, and the black waters of a lake, all
inscribed in two square centimeters.

The anecdote includes a wealth of credible details: the precision of
the date, its chronological relationship to the history of the Eastman-Kodak
Company—George Eastman invented photographic film in 1889—the
geographical accuracy—Rochester is indeed on Lake Ontario—the precise
quantities of cameras, film, and plates destroyed, the professions of the
sect's founders, the approximate date of its founding, the date and author of
the novel based on the incident, and the precise number of victims.

Two details, presented offhandedly in the middle and at the end of
the story of the painting, confer upon it an importance which distinguishes
this painting from the other 150 described in the novel: Heinrich Kürz
became an artist in order to paint "Les Ensorcelés du lac Ontario"; his father
was one of the seventy-eight victims of the incident it portrays. (Kürz
would have been seven at the time.)

The martyred sectarians, referred to as victims, were iconoclasts in
the original sense of the term, image breakers. Although the description

ignores their motivation, one can imagine that they chose to ransack "systematically" the Kodak offices and warehouses as a symbolic manifestation of their moral opposition to the newly created photographic industry; their destruction of cameras, plates, and film is in the tradition of the original eighth-century Byzantine iconoclasts. The citizens of Rochester, outraged by the attack upon their new industry, respond with unexpected zeal: half the citizens of the town chase the sectarians doggedly. Preferring death to capture, the iconoclasts jump into the waters of Lake Ontario; seventy-eight drown. The son of one of the fanatic iconoclasts becomes an artist in order to paint an image of their act. Let us ignore momentarily the apparent incongruity of young Kürz's decision and consider some personal but public facts which relate Georges Perec to Heinrich Kürz:[4]

1. Perec's Jewish parents were victims of the Nazi occupation and left him an orphan at age seven.

2. Perec began to write in order to commemorate the deaths of his parents.[5]

3. Perec achieves his greatest effects of imagination and virtuosity through constraint. It is not unreasonable to compare the creation of a painting on a surface 2 x 1 centimeter to the writing of a 300-page novel without using the letter E.

4. In all of his published novels, and most extensively in his masterpiece, *La Vie mode d'emploi,* of which *Un Cabinet d'amateur* is an offshoot, Perec grafts into his text quotations from dozens of authors. This process is analogous to Kürz's copying of paintings within "Un Cabinet d'amateur."

As we have seen, "Les Ensorcelés du lac Ontario" exists only as a miniature copy of an unrealized painting. The miniature itself enjoys only a very brief temporal existence. "Un Cabinet d'amateur," completed at the end of 1912, and first exhibited in April 1913, was at least partially destroyed on October 24, 1913, as the result of an incident which Perec qualifies as "inévitable": "Un visiteur exaspéré qui avait attendu toute la journée sans pouvoir entrer dans la salle, y fit soudain irruption et projeta contre le tableau le contenu d'une grosse bouteille d'encre de Chine, réussissant à prendre la fuite avant de se faire lyncher" (24). Unconsciously, but "inévitably" imitating the gesture of the sectarian sackers of the Eastman Kodak Factory, the lone terrorist, like his iconoclastic predecessors, flees the fury of a lynch mob. The outraged lovers of images, on one hand the Rochester mob seeking to avenge the destruction of cameras, on the other the thousands of admirers of Kürz's painting who crowd the exhibit daily, pursue the iconoclasts with a deadly fury.

The novel never reveals the extent of the damage caused by the "grosse bouteille" of ink. The painting is removed from the exhibit. Six months later, its owner, Hermann Raffke, dies, and the remains of the painting are entombed with the remains of the collector. All that survives are hundreds of Kürz's preliminary drawings and "une photographie médiocre, prise clandestinement par un des gardiens de la salle où le tableau avait été exposé" (62). The text does not tell us if the mediocre image was printed on Kodak paper.

The discussion of the iconoclastic attacks surrounding the creation and destruction of "Les Ensorcelés du lac Ontario" and "Un Cabinet d'amateur" suggests a certain circularity. Let us leave for a moment the notion of iconoclasm to pursue the notion of circularity, which will of course lead us directly back.

• • •

The painting within Kürz's "Un Cabinet d'amateur," which fascinated the public and which brought to the exhibit thousands of visitors armed with magnifying glasses, was not "Les Ensorcelés du lac Ontario," but rather "Un Cabinet d'amateur" itself. For among the dozens of pictures which appear upon the walls of the gallery painted by Kürz, occupying a central location is "Un Cabinet d'amateur," the painting within the painting, which again contains itself on an increasingly reduced scale "almost" infinitely. The original canvas measures two by three meters; each successive copy is approximately one-third the size of the preceding one; the eighth reproduction is a line, half a millimeter long.[6]

One further step in the "construction en abîme" is the arrangement of the exhibit hall, a life-size model of the painting, in which the Raffke Collection, including "Un Cabinet d'amateur," is displayed as in the painting. The interior of Hermann Raffke's tomb will later reproduce, on a much smaller scale, the arrangement of the exhibit hall.

The ever-increasing crowd of spectators, armed with their magnifying glasses, quickly discovered that the artist had not been satisfied to copy slavishly, over and over and smaller and smaller, the masterpieces of the Raffke Collection. On the contrary, he had cleverly brought modifications to each successive level, modifications which the visitors never tired of discovering: characters and details disappeared, changed place, were replaced by others. Some modifications were major: whole paintings disappeared. Others were barely noticeable: "La plume un peu délabrée d'un chapeau, deux rangs de perles au lieu de trois, la couleur d'un ruban, la forme d'une écuelle, la poignée d'une épée, le dessin d'un lustre" (23). In addition, Kürz discreetly introduced all of the members of the Raffke family into the painting at various levels of the copied portraits.

The "anonymous" entry in the catalog of the exhibit describing "Un Cabinet d'amateur" dwells on the effect of the painting's circularity:

> Un Cabinet d'amateur n'est pas seulement la représentation anecdotique d'un musée particulier; par le jeu de ces reflets successifs, par le charme quasi magique qu'opèrent ces répétitions de plus en plus minuscules, c'est une œuvre qui bascule dans un univers proprement onirique où son pouvoir de séduction s'amplifie jusqu'à l'infini, et où la précision exacerbée de la matière picturale, loin d'être sa propre fin, débouche tout à coup sur la Spiritualité de l'Eternel Retour. (20)

Art critic Lester Nowak, in an article published just after the close of the exhibit, interprets negatively the circularity of "Un Cabinet d'amateur." In the painting's repetitions and reflections of itself, Nowak finds rather than the infinite expansion of an eternal cycle, "une image de la mort de l'art, un réflexion spéculaire sur ce monde condamné à la répétition infinie de ces propres modèles" (28). He dismisses the playful variations introduced throughout the repetitions as "l'expression ultime de la mélancolie de l'artiste" (29). They represent a false freedom, a failed attempt to trouble the established order of art and to escape the narrow boundaries dictated by the forced return.

One other painting exhibited as part of the Raffke Collection and occupying a privileged position in both the exhibit and "Un Cabinet d'amateur" attracts Nowak's attention. Mounted on an easel in the right hand corner of the exhibit and just opposite the seated collector is the "Portrait de Bronco McGinnis" who exhibited himself at the Chicago World's Fair as "l'homme le plus tatoué du monde." The portrait is the work of German-American artist Adolphus Kleidröst, who began his career in Cologne before moving to Cleveland. Nowak finds in the portrait a powerful symbol in support of his contention that "Un Cabinet d'amateur" is an image of the death of art:

Et peut-être n'y avait-il rien de plus poignant et de plus risible dans cette œuvre que cet homme monstrueusement tatoué, ce corps peint qui semblait monter la garde devant chaque ressassement du tableau: homme devenu peinture sous le regard du collectionneur, symbole nostalgique et dérisoire, ironique et désabusé de ce "créateur" dépossédé du droit de peindre, désormais voué à regarder et à offrir en spectacle la seule prouesse d'une surface intégralement peinte. (29)

This "Portrait of the Artist as Painting" depicts, in Nowak's view, the ultimate misery of the artist, doubly condemned to observe and to be observed, but stripped of his right to create. Circumstances will later deprive this degraded image of the artist of its prominent position. Another portrait replaces it on the easel in the right hand corner of Hermann Raffke's tomb, a portrait of Raffke himself as a young man. (McGinnis himself, according to the text, had died in 1902. At that time it was discovered that he was really a Breton named Le Marech' and that only the tattoos on his chest were authentic.)

Nowak revises his interpretation of "Un Cabinet d'amateur" in a thesis on the works of Kürz published ten years after his article. In his thesis, Nowak finds in the reproduction and modification of works from the past, "un processus d'incorporation...un accaparement: en même temps projection vers l'autre, et Vol, au sens prométhéen du terme" (64). Nonetheless, between vision and representation are inscribed the fragile boundaries which constitute the limits of creativity, "et dont le développement ultime ne peut être que le Silence, ce silence volontaire et auto-destructeur que Kürz s'est imposé après avoir achevé cette œuvre" (65).

The painting's circular returns upon itself, no longer seen as a futile exercise in self-reanimation, but rather as a conscious assumption of the history and substance of art, symbolize the artist's decision to carry with him on his search for new territory the heavy heritage of the past. This heritage establishes the limits of art, tracing the narrow boundaries of creativity, whose ultimate development, in an increasingly rarefied realm of possibilities, is silence. The artist's silence is distinguished from the passive death of art evoked in the earlier article; it is a voluntary and significant act of self-destruction. The creator of images becomes iconoclastic.

Un Cabinet d'amateur is George Perec's last published novel. But this is more an accident of fate than evidence of the silence and self-destruction evoked in the novel. The text carries within itself, however, a violent, willful form of iconoclasm through which the plot destroys itself and leaves nothing in its wake. In the last two pages of the novel, we learn with vertiginous rapidity that

1. Most of the paintings in the Raffke Collection were fakes, painted by Raffke's nephew Humbert.

2. The exhibition and sale of the paintings were part of an elaborate plot involving forged paintings, faked papers, and manufactured evidence of authenticity.

3. Heinrich Kürz never existed; "Un Cabinet d'amateur" and the other paintings attributed to him were also the work of Humbert Raffke.

4. Art critic Lester Nowak was part of the conspiracy and therefore presumably based his article and thesis on material he knew to be fraudulent.

Perec concludes his novel, "Des vérifications entreprises avec diligence ne tardèrent pas à démontrer qu'en effet la plupart des tableaux de la collection Raffke étaient faux, comme sont la plupart des détails de ce récit fictif, conçu pour le seul plaisir, et le seul frisson, du faire-semblant" (90).

The novel's last sentence quite literally breaks the charm. The reader's willing suspension of disbelief, our all too eager readiness to give the fiction the benefit of all our accumulated doubts is ungraciously mocked. The corner of our minds that we had consciously silenced, in which, despite all of the credible details that Perec accumulates, we had timidly wondered whether or not Renoir had really painted a "Marchande de cigarettes," Cézanne a "Jeu de dominos," Rubens a "Midas et Apollon," and Vermeer a "Billet dérobé"—this skeptical corner of our minds is dramatically given the upper hand. And our more trusting, generous, literary imagination is disappointed.

In the first half of the last sentence it is merely the fictional strand which falls apart: all of the paintings are fakes; Raffke, Kürz, and Novak are charlatans. But something more dramatic happens in the last words of the novel: fiction itself falls apart; the author tells us not to believe what he tells us; he was just having fun. Not only are the paintings fakes and the characters frauds, but the fakes and frauds are fake fakes and fraudulent frauds.

The seemingly incongruous decision of young Heinrich Kürz to memorialize his martyred father by painting a picture commemorating his iconoclastic attack upon the Kodak Factory is tempered by the following considerations:

1. He never actually painted the picture.
2. The tiny copy of the unrealized painting was destroyed.
3. The painting in which the copy appears was interpreted as an image of the death of art.
4. Heinrich Kürz abandoned painting.
5. Georges Perec, who assumes the identity of Heinrich Kürz, successively destroys the painting, Kürz, and ultimately the novel in which Kürz and the painting appear.

• • •

Perec's only published short story, "Le Voyage d'hiver,"[7] which first appeared in 1979, resembles structurally *Un Cabinet d'amateur*. In place of Heinrich Kürz's painting, Perec presents Hugo Vernier's novel, *Le Voyage d'hiver*. Professor Vincent Degraël is at first mildly interested to note in this novel, which he discovered in the library of a friend's estate near Le Havre in 1939, phrases, lines, and passages which he recognizes as belonging to the works of some thirty late nineteenth-century writers including Mendès, Moréas, Villiers, Banville, Corbière, and Cros as well as Verlaine, Rimbaud, and Mallarmé. The young professor's interest turns to astonishment when he discovers that *Le Voyage d'hiver* was published in 1864, and that what he had first thought to be a pastiche is actually a previously unknown source for most of the major poets of the last half of the nineteenth century.

The war and his mobilization prevent Degraël from pursuing his discovery until 1945, by which time the copy of the novel he read had been destroyed along with his friend's estate during the bombing of Le Havre. He is unable to locate any other copies of the novel, which leads him to believe that "les cinq cents exemplaires de l'édition avaient été volontairement détruits par ceux-là même qui s'en étaient si directement inspirés" (36). He does find scattered traces of the book and its author. Hugo Vernier was born in 1836 in Vimy, Pas-de-Calais. His novel was published in 1864 by Hervé Frères in Valenciennes. In the correspondence of several authors, Degraël finds allusions to Hugo Vernier which other scholars had mistakenly identified as allusions to Victor Hugo.

Degraël spends thirty years, up to his death in the psychiatric hospital at Verrières, trying to assemble the documents which would permit him to publish his thesis and thereby rewrite the literary history of the nineteenth century. Following his death, his students find among the stacks of documents which line his study:

> un épais registre relié de toile noire et dont l'étiquette portait, soigneusement calligraphié, *Le Voyage d'hiver:* les huit premières pages retraçaient l'histoire de ces vaines recherches; les trois cent quatre-vingt-douze autres étaient blanches. (36)

The nearly empty notebook recalls Balzac's *Un Chef-d'œuvre inconnu* as well as Valène's empty outline sketch of the apartment building in *La Vie mode d'emploi.* The unfortunate, insane professor, like Dr. Dinteville of *La Vie mode d'emploi,* dreams of scholarly glory, of leaving a significant published trace of his life's activity. His fate echoes that of the remarkable Vernier (as well as that of Frenhoffer, Valène, and Dinteville). Deprived not only of glory, but also of existence, Degraël dies leaving only ambiguous and incomplete traces of his passage.

Harry Mathews compares the last paragraph of *Un Cabinet d'amateur* with the end of *La Vie mode d'emploi,* in which, "le livre est réduit à rien."[8] The search for an enduring artistic expression seems to come to a dead end, in fact encounters something much worse, self-destruction. The vanishing traces in Perec's last fiction—the almost blank canvas left by Valène, the revelation that Heinrich Kürz never existed, the failure of Vincent Degraël to prove the existence of Hugo Vernier—in conjunction with Perec's personal revelation that during the two years which followed the publication of *La Vie mode d'emploi* he wrote practically nothing and that all he wrote fell under the influence of *La Vie mode d'emploi,*[9] suggest a will, or at least a tendency, towards silence.

CONCLUSION

From amidst all the things, all the lives, all the stories which come streaming forth from the words and pictures created by Perec, one brief image assumes a life of its own, remains hauntingly imprinted upon the retina: the brief frames of "Récits d'Ellis Island," showing Perec himself studying the old yellowed photographs of an immigrant's scrapbook, looking for...

Almost the same image recurs near the beginning of both the fictional and autobiographical sections of *W ou le souvenir d'enfance,* the mature man searching through old photos, old documents, looking for...

The word which most often, but still imprecisely, translates the object of the search is *traces:* trace, trail, footprint, mark. A more concrete though still incomplete expression of the object of the search appears in the final paragraphs of *Espèces d'espaces:*

> Mon pays natal, le berceau de ma famille, la maison où je serais né, l'arbre que j'aurais vu grandir... le grenier de mon enfance empli de souvenirs intacts... (122)

The missing sought-after element is continuity, the uninterrupted flow of time and space through countless generations, the undefinable transmissions from generation to generation which normally accompany the transmission of genes. "Une seule chose m'était précisément interdite: celle de naître dans le pays de mes ancêtres...et d'y grandir dans la continuité d'une tradition..." ("Récits d'Ellis Island," 44).

In *Les Choses* and *Un Homme qui dort,* what is missing from the lives of the protagonists is never clearly understood or expressed. Jérôme, Sylvie, and the young student are misfits, *parias, bannis,* looking for more than the life they thought they had chosen can offer. They seek to order their environment, to impose their wills, but are ultimately undone by the unaccommodating, refractory nature of the building blocks of Perec's fictional universe: time and space.

Anton Voyl is the only one of Perec's protagonists to have a clear intuitive sense that something is missing from his life, that he is cursed. It matters not that what is missing from his universe is an arbitrarily chosen letter; his search is nonetheless fervent, his alienation nonetheless anguished, his disappearance nonetheless tragic.

Percival Bartlebooth, independent, self-exiled, alone, conceives an immensely complicated project for which he has no particular predisposition. The goal of his project is the traceless, self-annihilating manipulation of time and space through the construction of puzzles. His motivation, his need to pursue relentlessly a gratuitous, empty exercise, is never explained. He travels the world for twenty years, painting ports. For twenty more years he reconstructs the scenes he has painted become puzzles, before sending the reconstituted puzzles on to their dissolution to complete the project's circularity. Space—the ports he visited and whose images he sends forward through time to his old age—is fragmented, reconstituted, and annihilated as part of a process which Bartlebooth defends vigorously and whose essential *raison d'être* can only be an instinctive, unreasoned need to control the fragmentation of time and space.

Valène's motivation is more conscious, his project more fragile, psychologically more dangerous: "L'idée même de ce tableau qu'il projetait de faire et dont les images étalées, éclatées, s'étaient mises à hanter le moindre de ses instants" (168). The proliferating time and space of the apartment building resist the cataloging tendency of his artistic vision, his need to contain its life within carefully outlined squares.

Lost traces, fragmentation, the obsessive ordering of time and space—these images haunt Perec's fiction and autobiography. For Perec and his alter-egos the smooth continuity of time and space is interrupted; the round faultless eternity which Perec imagines in "L'Eternité" is flawed by folds, by lacks. disappearances, cuts, separations, by the absences which haunt his life and his work.

Perec's literary career itself was cut short by his untimely death. The apparent silence which followed *La Vie mode d'emploi,* interrupted by the short, disturbing fictions, *Un Cabinet d'amateur* and "Le Voyage d'hiver," gives the false impression that Perec had little more to write. Nothing could be further from the truth; according to Bernard Magné there remains as much unpublished material as published.[1] Death surprised Perec as he struggled to finish the novel *53 Jours,* a dazzlingly complex project which Perec conceived as an ultimate resolution of the search for continuity, inspired by a sentence from Saint-Réal which Stendhal quotes as an epigraph to chapter 13 of *Le Rouge et le noir,* "Un roman: c'est un miroir qu'on promène le long d'un chemin." *53 Jours,* through a series of spectral and symmetrical constructions telling a story of the Resistance and using references to the life and works of Stendhal, was intended to present a complete and harmonious fictional universe. From the page of notes which, in addition to the completed manuscript pages, Perec left, a sentence emerges, translating his desire for wholeness: "Pas de faille nulle part."[2]

Pending the publication of Perec's incomplete novel of wholeness, any conclusion on the works of Perec must be tentative, itself incomplete. The fictional universe of Georges Perec yearns for completeness. The not yet completed Perec puzzle strives to order its pieces, to eliminate the cutmarks, in order to recapture an Edenic, virginal wholeness. It is ironic and disturbing that legal complications have delayed the publication of *53 Jours,* that even after his death, Perec's search for wholeness encounters the resistance of fragmentation, that the ultimate traces of his passage are at least temporarily suspended.

NOTES

Introduction

[1]Perec lists them in his "Bibliographie sommaire," in *L'Arc* 76 (1979): 96.

[2]*Cause Commune,* founded by Perec, Jean Duvignaud, and Paul Virilio. The first issue was published in May 1972.

[3]Jean Duvignaud, "George Perec, prix Renaudot 1965," *Le Nouvel Observateur* 54 (24-30 Nov. 1965): 27.

[4]Paulette Perec, personal interview, 20 June 1985, Paris. Marcel Bénabou in "Perec et la Judéité," *Cahiers Georges Perec,* I (Paris: POL, 1985), p. 21, describes Perec's student years in terms of a search for political and philosophical roots: "C'est l'époque de la *Ligne générale* (nom d'une revue d'analyse marxiste que Georges Perec et ses amis souhaitaient fonder vers 1958)... c'est une époque surtout marquée par la fascination pour le marxisme et la révolution, par la recherche de la justice en actes, par le goût de l'universel."

[5]George Perec, *Espéces d'espaces* (Paris: Galilée, 1974), p. 123.

Chapter 1

[1]Georges Perec, *Les Choses* (Paris: Julliard, 1965). All references are to this edition.

[2]Jean Duvignaud, "Effet d'éloignement par rapport aux choses," *L'Arc* 76 (1979): 24.

[3]Robert Kanters, "Les Choses et les mots," *Le Figaro Littéraire* 20.1023 (25 Nov. 1965): 5.

[4]Jean Chalon, "Georges Perec, l'homme sans qui 'les choses' ne seraient pas ce qu'elles sont," *Le Figaro Littéraire* 20.1023 (25 Nov. 1965): 3. In Georges Perec, "Emprunts à Flaubert," *L'Arc* 79 (1980): 49, Perec lists seven specific borrowings from Flaubert in *Les Choses*. John Pedersen in *Perec ou les textes croisés* (Copenhagen: University of Copenhagen, 1985), p. 39, also discusses borrowings from Flaubert in *Les Choses*.

[5]The Chalon interview mentioned above and Jean Duvignaud, "Le Bonheur de la modernité," *Le Nouvel Observateur* 15 Dec. 1965: 32-33.

[6]Janick Arbois, "Les choses et la vie," *Signes du Temps* 1, Jan. 1966: 32.

[7]Duvignaud, "Le Bonheur," p. 32.

[8]In the Duvignaud interview cited above, Perec states: "Il y a une distinction très simple entre le nouveau roman et ce que j'ai essayé de faire. Robbe-Grillet est tout entier du côté du langage 'dénoté' (comme dit Roland Barthes) et moi, je serais tout entier du côté du langage qui entoure les choses, de ce qu'il y a en dessous, de tout ce qui les nourrit, de tout ce qu'on leur injecte.

[9]Annie Leclerc, *"Les Choses:* un combat malheureux," *Les Temps modernes* 21.235 (Dec. 1965): 1135.

[10]Arbois, p. 32.

[11]Henri Peretz, *"Les Choses:* un combat malheureux," *Les Temps modernes* 21.235 (Dec. 1965): 1135.

[12]Georges Perec, *Quel petit vélo à guidon chromé au fond de la cour?* (Paris: Denoël, 1966). All references are to this edition.

[13]Anne Roche in "L'Auto(bio)graphie," *Cahiers Georges Perec*, I (Paris: POL, 1985), pp. 68-70, refers to *Ligne Générale* and other autobiographical references in *Quel petit vélo*.

[14]Yvan Andouart, "Roule petit vélo," *Le Canard Enchaîné* 51.2365 (16 Feb. 1966): 7.

[15]In the original edition, the page references of the index are in error. The page numbers are corrected in a subsequent edition (Folio #1413).

[16]The young soldier's name goes through several comic transformations: Karamanlis, Karaschoff, Karabinowicz, Karamagnole, Karachose, Karafalk, Karastenberger, Karaniette, Karamel, Karabine, etc.

[17]Harry Mathews, "Le Catalogue d'une vie," *Magazine Littéraire* 193 (Mar. 1983): 15.

[18]Robert Kanters, "Aux écoutes de la nuit," *Figaro Littéraire* 21.1035 (17 Feb. 1966): 5.

[19]Duvignaud, "Le Bonheur," p. 32.

[20]Georges Perec, *Un Homme qui dort* (Paris: Denoël, 1967). All references are to this edition.

[21]Marc Slonim, "Sleeper," *The New York Times Book Review* 18 June 1967: 38.

[22]John Gilbert, *"Un Homme qui dort," Novel* 2.1 (Fall 1968): 94-96.

[23]Etienne Lalou, "Un déserteur de l'histoire," *L'Express* 829 (8 May 1967): 40.

[24]Bernard Pingaud, "L'Indifférence, passion méconnue," *Quinzaine Littéraire* 27 (1-15 May 1967): 3.

[25]Warren F. Motte, Jr., in *The Poetics of Experiment, A Study of the Works of Georges Perec* (Lexington: French Forum Publishers, 1984), p. 42, notes nine references to dirty socks in *Un Homme qui dort* and three more in *La Boutique obscure.*

[26]Marcel Proust, *Du côté de chez Swann* (Paris: Gallimard Folio, 1954), p. 11.

[27]See pages 152-53. In a letter written to Denise Getzler, published in *Littératures* 7 (Spring 1983): 63, Perec expresses his admiration for Melville's short story: *"Bartleby* a ceci de particulier qu'il est, pour moi, tout entier contenu dan ce sentiment trouble—l'étrangeté, l'éloignement, l'irrémédiable, l'inachevable, le vide, etc.,—et qu'il en est l'expression, à ma connaissance, la plus achevée."

[28]Proust, p. 11.

[29]Claude Burgelin in "Perec et la Cruauté," *Cahiers Georges Perec,* I (Paris: POL, 1985), pp. 33-37, discusses the imagery of this section of *Un Homme qui dort.*

[30]Pedersen, p. 48, interprets the protagonist's fear as a positive step towards acceptance of his relation to the world.

Chapter 2

[1]Georges Perec, *La Disparition* (Paris: Denoël, 1969). Subsequent references are to this edition.

[2]See Oulipo, *La Littérature potentielle* (Paris: Gallimard, 1973). In this volume Perec republishes the postscript to *La Disparition* and "Histoire du Lipogramme."

[3]Larousse definition cited by Perec in Oulipo, p. 78.

[4]See Raymond Roussel, *Comment j'ai écrit certains de mes livres* (Paris: Jean-Jacques Pauvert, 1963), pp. 11-12. Perec translates Roussel's sentence, "Les lettres du blanc sur les bandes du vieux billard," as "L'inscription du blanc sur un bord du billard," which reappears as "L'inscription du blanc sur un corbillard."

[5]Warren Motte in "Embellir les lettres," *Cahiers Georges Perec,* I (Paris: POL, 1985), p. 115, makes the same point.

[6]Etienne Lalou, "320 pages sans la lettre E," *L'Express* 28 April 1969: 57.

[7]John Lee, "Brise ma rime," *Littératures* 7 (Spring 1983): 11-20, studies the transformation of Mallarmé's "Brise Marine" in *La Disparition.*

[8]Jacques Derrida, *La Dissémination* (Paris: Seuil, 1972), p. 32.

[9]Alain Robbe-Grillet, *Le Miroir qui revient* (Paris: Minuit, 1984), p. 214.

[10]Bernard Magné, "Le Puzzle, mode d'emploi, petite propédeutique à une lecture métatextuelle de *La Vie mode d'emploi* de Georges Perec," *Texte* I (1982): 84-86, discusses the dynamic potential of absences in Perec's work.

[11]Marcel Bénabou, "Autour d'une absence," *Quinzaine Littéraire* 72 (1-15 May 1969): 9.

[12]Judith Gollub, "Georges Perec et la Litterature Potentielle," *The French Review* XLV.6 (May 1972): 1100.

[13]Perec, in keeping with his obsession, has transformed Van Vogt's title, *La saga du* Ā. The Roubaud article in Oulipo is called Ɛ . The symbol of Christian Bourgois is ꙅ , which is composed of three incomplete 6's, and which, if completed, would yield three E's.

[14]Georges Perec, *W ou le souvenir d'enfance* (Paris: Denoël, 1975).

[15]Ewa Pawlikowska, "La colle bleue de Gaspard Winckler," *Littératures* 7 (Spring 1983): 81. Pedersen, pp. 61-62, discusses as part of this tendency to show traces, Perec's occasional failures to deal perfectly with the constraints of *La Disparition;* for him, the "clinamen" is an intentional trace of the artist's effort.

[16]Perec, *W,* p. 59. See Motte, "Embellir les lettres, " p. 118, for an illuminating discussion of the relationship between *W* and *La Disparition.* Pedersen, p. 64, notes that the words *père* and *mère* necessarily disappear from *La Disparition.*

[17]Georges Perec, *Les Revenentes* (Paris: Julliard, 1972). All references are to this edition.

[18]Oulipo, pp. 101-06.

[19]In *La Littérature Potentielle,* Perec publishes, in addition to the postscript to *La Disparition,* "Histoire du Lipogramme," and "Palindrome," the transformations of poems by Rimbaud and Baudelaire contained in *La Disparition;* "Drame alphabétique," a very short play in which the spoken lines are nothing more than the letters of the alphabet, in order, joined into words ("Abbesse: Aidez!"); "Le Petit abécédaire illustré," a series of short descriptive texts, published with their key ("Dad est dit dodu." "Rare est rire aux rues."); and two contributions coauthored with Marcel Bénabou.
In *Atlas de littérature potentielle* (Paris: Gallimard, 1981), Perec publishes the poem "Ulcérations," the article, "Quatre figures pour *La Vie mode d'emploi,*" and several short texts.
In *La Bibliothèque Oulipienne* (Geneva: Slatkine, 1981) are republished "Ulcérations," "DOS, CADDY D'AISSELLES," and "Le Petit abécédaire illustré." Perec also collaborated on several exercises of the final volume grouped under the title "La Cantatrice Sauve."

Chapter 3

[1]Georges Perec, "Notes sur ce que je cherche," *Le Figaro,* 8 Dec. 1978: 28.

[2]Anne Roche, "Auto(bio)graphie," *Cahiers Georges Perec* I (Paris: POL, 1985), pp. 65-80.

[3]Georges Perec, *W ou le souvenir d'enfance* (Paris: Denoël, 1975). All references are to this edition. In the second chapter of the book, Perec explains that he originally created the story of W when he was thirteen and then forgot about it. With the aid of rediscovered drawings he rewrote and published the story in 1969 and 1970 in *La Quinzaine littéraire.* Four years later he conceived the project of publishing the story with his autobiography.

[4]The book was the subject of a 1987 public seminar at the Université de Paris VII.

[5]Bernard Pingaud, "Ceci n'est pas un puzzle," *L'Arc* 76 (1979): 1.

[6]David Rousset, *L'Univers concentrationnaire* (Paris: Gallimard, 1967).

[7]Claude Burgelin, *"W ou le souvenir d'enfance* de Georges Perec," *Les Temps modernes* 31.351 (1975): 568-71.

[8]Catherine Clément, "Auschwitz ou la disparition," *L'Arc* 76 (1979): 87-90.

[9]Robert Misrahi, *"W,* un roman reflexif," *L'Arc* 76 (1979): 81-86.

[10]Jean-Baptiste Baronian, "'*W* par Georges Perec," *Magazine Littéraire,* 103-04 (Sept. 1975): 255-56.

[11]Misrahi, pp. 81-82.

[12]Burgelin, pp. 568-69.

[13]Philippe Berthier, "Georges Perec, *W ou le souvenir d'enfance,*" *Le Bulletin des Lettres* 370 (15 July 1975): 255-56.

[14]Claude Burgelin, "Perec et la Curauté," *Cahiers Georges Perec* I (Paris: POL, 1985), pp. 37-39, discusses the sadistic imagery of *W ou le souvenir d'enfance*.

[15]Burgelin, *"W ou le souvenir d" enfance,"* p. 571.

[16]Anne Roche, "SouWenir d'enfance," *Magazine Littéraire* (March 1983): 27.

[17]Jean-Baptiste Mauroux, "Georges Perec, *W ou le souvenir d'enfance,"* *Quinzaine Littéraire* 211 (1-15 June 1975): 11.

[18]Matthieu Galey, "Perec: des Mémoires en charpie," *L'Express* (28 July 1975): 16-17.

[19]Alain Poirson, "Georges Perec, *W ou le souvenir d'enfance,"* *Pensée* 187 (June 1976): 152.

[20]George Perec, *La Boutique obscure* (Paris: Denoël, 1973). All references are to this edition. As the pages are not numbered, reference numbers in the text will refer to the number of the dream. For a discussion of the psychoanalytical sessions which lead to Perec's interest in his own dreams, see Georges Perec, "Les Lieux d'une ruse," *Cause Commune* I (Paris: 10/18, 1977): 77-78.

[21]Maurice Achard, *"La Boutique obscure,"* *Combat* (4 July 1973).

[22]Claude Bonnefoy, "Le Souvenir et le rêve," *Nouvelles Littéraires* 51.2389 (1-16 July 1973): 7.

[23]Roger Bastide, "Postface," first page.

[24]Bastide, fifth page.

[25]André Marissel, "Georges Perec: *La Boutique obscure,"* *Esprit* 435 (May 1974): 909.

[26]Claude Mauriac, "Matière première onirique et production littéraire," *Le Figaro Littéraire* 1422 (18 August 1973), Part II: 8.

[27]Catherine David, "La Chambre Noire," *Le Nouvel Observateur* 461 (10-16 Sept. 1973): 53.

[28]Georges Perec, *Espèces d'espaces* (Paris: Galilée, 1974). All references are to this edition.

[29]Claude-Henri Rocquet, "A la recherche de l'espace perdu," *Quinzaine Littéraire* 199 (1-15 Dec. 1974): 24.

[30]Georges Perec, "Tentative d'épuisement d'un lieu parisien," *Le Pourissement des Sociétés,* No. 1/75 of *Cause Commune* (Paris: Union générale d'éditions, 1975). The article was published separately as a book (Paris: Christian Bourgois, 1982). The article was originally intended as part of the project described in the next paragraph.

[31]Perec, "Tentative," p. 12.

[32]Georges Perec, "Notes concernant les objets qui sont sur ma table de travail," *Nouvelles Littéraires* 2521 (26 Feb. 1976): 17.

[33]Professor Jean Marieu, University of Bordeaux, personal interview, 1 December 1984.

[34]Georges Perec, *Je me souviens* (Paris: Hachette, 1978). All references are to this edition. Numbers in the text refer to the number of the memory (and not the page) unless otherwise noted.

[35]Georges Perec, "Ce qu'il se passe quand il ne se passe rien, *Le Monde* 10274 (10 Feb. 1978): 17.

[36]Monique Pétillon, "Les 'choses vues' de Georges Perec," *Le Monde* 10274 (10 Feb. 1978): 17.

[37]Chantal Labre, *"Je me souviens," Esprit,* II.3 (Nov. -Dec. 1978): 104.

[38]Serge Koster, "Quand le 'je' se change en nous," *Quinzaine Littéraire* 273 (16-28 Feb. 1978): 7.

[39]Georges Perec, "Ce qu'il se passe."

[40]Labre, p. 104.

[41]Perec, *W,* p. 14.

Chapter 4

[1]Georges Perec, *Alphabets* (Paris: Galilée, 1976). All references are to this edition. See Warren J. Motte, Jr., *The Poetics of Experiment* (Lexington: French Forum, 1984), pp. 18-29, for an extremely valuable discussion of the formal aspects of all of Perec's poetry.

[2]Georges Perec, *La Clôture et autres poèmes* (Paris: Hachette, 1980). All references are to this edition.

[3]Robin Buss, "Eleven Times Tables," *Times Literary Supplement* 3921 (6 May 1977): 553.

[4]Mireille Ribière, "Coup d'L," *Littératures* 7 (Spring 1983): 49-60. See also Ribière's article, "Alphabets," *Cahiers Georges Perec,* I (Paris: POL, 1985), pp. 134-45, for analyses of poems 104, 41, 26, and 91.

[5]Harry Mathews, "Le Catalogue d'une vie," *Magazine Littéraire* 193 (March 1983): 16.

[6]Emmanuel Hocquard and Raquel, *Orange Export Ltd. 1969-1986* (Paris: Flammarion, 1986), pp. 249-50. As well as the original Orange Export Ltd. edition of the poem, there also exists a version with a misprint published in *Magazine Littéraire* 193 (March 1983): 35.

[7]Georges Perec et Jean-Marie Le Sidaner, "Entretien," *L'Arc* 76 (1979): 8.

[8]In "Entretien avec Patrice Fardeau," in *France Nouvelle,* No. 1744, cited by Benoît Peeters in "Echafaudages," *Cahiers Georges Perec* I (Paris: POL, 1985), p. 179, Perec complains, "dans *Alphabets,* les lecteurs n'ont pratiquement jamais lu les poèmes comme des poèmes... mais comme des exploits." Peeters responds, "Si les lecteurs n'avaient pas connu la contrainte, ils n'auraient sans doute rien lu du tout."

[9]*Die Maschine* (Stuttgart: Reclam, 1972), *Tagstimmen* (Sarrebruck, 1971), *Konzertstück für Sprecher und Orchester* (Sarrebruck, 1972). See Motte, *op. cit.,* pp. 118-19, for a discussion of *Die Maschine.*

[10]"Fonctionnement du système nerveux dans la tête," *Cause Commune* 3 (1972): 42-55. "Le Petit abécédaire illustré." "Dimuendo." "Souvenir d'un voyage à Thouars." "Tentative de description de choses vues au carrefour Mabillon le 19 mai, 1978." Atelier de Création Radiophonique, 381 (25 Feb. 1979). These titles with some additional commentary appear in Perec's annotated bibliography in *L'Arc* 76 (1979): 91-96.

[11]Georges Perec, *Théâtre I* (Paris: Hachette, 1981).

[12]Quoted in Colette Godard, "Avant-première: Comment fonctionne la machine?" *Lettres Françaises* 1323 (25 Feb.-3 March 1970): 13.

[13]Bertrand Poirot-Delpech, " 'L'Augmentation' de Georges Perec," *Le Monde* 7819 (4 March 1970): 21.

[14]Motte, pp. 120-22, discusses Perec's borrowings in *La Poche Parmentier.*

[15]Michel Cournot, *"La Poche Parmentier,* de Georges Perec à Nice," *Le Monde* 9053 (22 Feb. 1974): 23.

[16]They are listed in the Bibliography of *L'Arc,* cited above.

[17]Mireille Amiel, "Un Homme qui dort," *Cinéma 74* 187 (May 1974): 115.

[18]Georges Franju, "Au point mort de sa vie (sur un homme qui dort)," *Positif* 159 (May 1974): 57.

[19]Georges Perec and Robert Bober, "Récits d'Ellis Island," Institut National de l'Audiovisuel, Paris, 1980. There exists a published text with the same title (Paris: Sorbier, 1980).

[20]Alain Corneau, dir., *Série Noire,* scenario by Alain Corneau and Georges Perec, Gaumont, 1979. The complete text of the film was published in *L'Avant-Scène/Cinéma* 233 (1979).

[21]Jim Thompson, *A Hell of a Woman* (Berkeley: Creative Arts, 1954).

Chapter 5

[1]Georges Perec, *La Vie mode d'emploi* (Paris: Hachette, 1978). All references are to this edition. The subsequent Livre de Poche edition has the same pagination.

[2]John Pedersen, *Perec ou les textes croisés* (Copenhagen: University of Copenhagen, 1985), pp. 61-62, discusses (and defines) the "clinamen" as signature.

[3]In Georges Perec, "Emprunts à Flaubert," *L'Arc* 79 (1980): 49, Perec identifies the source of M. Gouttman as a "négociant usurier en articles de piété que Bouvard et Pécuchet rencontrent."

[4]Both Alain Goulet in *"La Vie mode d'emploi,* archives en jeu," *Cahiers Georges Perec* I (Paris: POL, 1985), p. 210, and John Pedersen in *Perec ou les textes croisés,* p. 103, comment on this and other "demonic" motifs which surround Winckler.

[5]There have been many studies of the importance of the puzzle motif in *La Vie mode d'emploi.* The best is Bernard Magné, "Le Puzzle, mode d'emploi, petite propédeutique à une lecture métatextuelle de *La Vie mode d'emploi* de Georges Perec," *Texte* I (1982): 71-96.

[6]Georges Perec and Gabriel Simony, "Entretien avec Georges Perec," *Jungle* 6 (15 Jan. 1983): 79.

[7]*Ibid.,* p. 76.

[8]Georges Perec, "La Maison des romans," *Magazine Littéraire* 141 (Oct. 1978): 35.

[9]Georges Perec, "Quatre Figures pour *La Vie mode d'emploi*," *L'Arc* 76 (1979): 51.

[10]Televised interview, *Apostrophes,* with Bernard Pivot, January 1979, Antenne 2.

[11]*L'Arc,* pp. 51-52. "Il s'agit de faire parcourir à un cheval les 64 cases d'un échiquier sans jamais s'arrêter plus d'une fois sur la même case. Il existe des milliers de solutions dont certaines, telle celle d'Euler, forment de surcroît des carrés magiques. Dans le cas particulier de *La Vie mode d'emploi,* il fallait trouver une solution pour un échiquier de 10 x 10. J'y suis parvenu par tâtonnements, d'une manière plutôt miraculeuse. La division du livre en six parties provient du même principe: chaque fois que le cheval est passé par les quatre bords du carré, commence une nouvelle partie." See also, Bernard Magné, "Cinquième Figure pour *La Vie mode d'emploi*," *Cahiers* I: 173-77, for a discussion of the "pseudo-quenine d'ordre 10."

[12]Perec, "Quatre Figures," p. 35.

[13]Georges Perec, "Des règles pour être libre," *Les Nouvelles Littéraires* 2575 (10 March 1977): 21.

[14]Georges Perec, "Un livre pour jouer avec," *Le Monde* 10471 (29 Sept. 1978): 18.

[15]Eugen Helmlé, "Traduire *La Vie mode d'emploi,*" *Littératures* 83 (Spring, 1983): 100.

[16]Oulipo, *Atlas de Littérature Potentielle* (Paris: Gallimard, 1981), pp. 394-95.

[17]Ewa Pawlikowska, "La colle bleue de Gaspard Winckler," *Littératures* 7 (Spring 1983): 80.

[18]Bernard Magné, "Noms naufragés," *Littératures* 7: 141-50.

[19]Bernard Magné, "Quelques problèmes de l'énonciation du régime fictionnel: l'exemple de *La Vie mode d'emploi* de Georges Perec," *Actes du Colloque d'Albi* (Albi: Ecole Normale d'Albi, 1982): 229-45. In his article, "Emprunts à Flaubert," Perec discusses his borrowings from Flaubert. Critics, with the help of Perec's notebooks, will undoubtedly eventually find all of the quotes. Benoît Peeters in "Echafaudages," *Cahiers* I: 185-86, questions the usefulness of these attempts to unravel Perec's "jeu citationnel."

[20]Perec, "Un livre pour jouer avec."

[21]Perec and Simony, "Entretien," p. 76.

[22]In "Emprunts à Flaubert," Perec reveals that several elements of the painting are borrowed from Flaubert. John Pedersen in *Perec ou les textes croisés,* p. 103, discusses the painting, with reference to the notion of "frame": windows, mirrors, paintings.

[23]Magné in "Quelques problèmes," discusses to what extent the reader may consider Valène to be the narrator of the novel.

[24]Jean-Pierre Vélis, "L'Homme créateur," *L'Education* 363 (12 Oct. 1978): 26.

[25]Perec, "Un livre pour jouer avec."

[26]Goulet, p. 203.

[27]Ewa Pawlikowska in "Citation, prise d'écriture," *Cahiers* I: 218 and 222, and Bernard Magné in "Lavis, mode d'emploi," *Cahiers* I: 241,

relate Valène's vision and Bartlebooth's puzzlemaking to Perec's use of implicit quotations; his grafting of texts from disparate sources to form a unified structure with invisible seams parallels the efforts of Bartlebooth and Valène.

Chapter 6

[1]Georges Perec, *Un Cabinet d'amateur* (Paris: Balland, 1979).

[2]Georges Perec and Gabriel Simony, "Entretien avec Georges Perec," *Jungle* 6 (15 Jan. 1983): 86. Bernard Magné in "Quelques Problèmes de l'énonciation en régime fictionnel: l'exemple de *La Vie mode d'emploi* de Georges Perec," *Actes du Colloque d'Albi* (Albi: Ecole Normale d'Albi, 1982): 245, explains that the paintings which are given a catalog number are generated, often by an obscure detail, by the chapter of *La Vie* which has the same number as the catalog number.

[3]Lanie Goodman in *"Un Cabinet d'amateur:* an Optical Disillusion," *Sub-Stance* 29 (1981): 110, identifies "les ensorcelés du lac Ontario" as one of the "tableaux vivants" in *Impressions d'Afrique.*

[4]Anne Roche in "L'Auto(bio)graphie," *Cahiers Georges Perec* I (Paris: POL, 1985): 76-78, includes *Un Cabinet d'amateur* among Perec's autobiographical works because of the parallels between the lives of Perec and Heinrich Kürz.

[5]See Perec's *W ou le souvenir d'enfance* (Paris: Denoël, 1975), p. 59.

[6]For a thorough discussion of the technique of "mise en abîme," see Lucien Dällenbach, *Le Récit spéculaire: Essai sur la mise en abîme* (Paris: Seuil, 1977), or the chapter entitled "Interior Duplication," in Bruce Morrissette, *Novel and Film: Essays in Two Genres* (Chicago: University of Chicago Press, 1985), pp. 141-56. John Pedersen in *Perec ou les textes croisés* (Copenhagen: University of Copenhagen, 1985), p. 106, discusses interior duplications in *La Vie mode d'emploi.*

[7]Georges Perec, "Le Voyage d'hiver," in *Saisons* (Paris: Hachette, 1979), "plaquette" edited by Nicole Vitoux. It was republished in *Magazine Littéraire* 193 (March 1983): 33-36. References are to the *Magazine Littéraire* edition. See Claudette Oriol-Boyer, "Le Voyage d'hiver," in *Cahiers Georges Perec* I (Paris: POL, 1985), pp. 146-70, for a discussion of the story. The *Cahiers* also include among the "Pièces Originales" a "Manuscrit préparatoire" for the story.

[8]Harry Mathews, "Le catalogue d'une vie," *Magazine Littéraire* 193 (March 1983): 20.

[9]In the *Jungle* interview, Perec gives examples of the obsessive presence of *La Vie mode d'emploi* in his subsequent literary projects.

Conclusion

[1]Bernard Magné, personal interview, 16 June 1985, Toulouse.

[2]Magné interview. In his interview in *Jungle* 6 (15 Jan. 1983): 82-83, perec comments on *53 Jours:* "C'est un peu comme si on mettait un livre dans un miroir et puis, ce que l'on voit de l'autre côté du miroir, c'est le contraire. C'est l'image inverse. C'est un livre où on va imaginer des choses dans la première partie et où dans la deuxième tout ce que l'on a imaginé va être complètement renversé."

BIBLIOGRAPHY

Achard, Maurice. *"La Boutique obscure." Combat* 4 July 1973: 23.

Amiel, Mireille. *"Un Homme qui dort." Cinéma 74* 187 (1974): 115.

Andouard, Yvan. "Roule petit vélo." *Le Canard Enchaîné* 16 Feb. 1966: 7.

Arbois, Janick. "Les Choses et la vie." *Signes du Temps* 1 (1966): 32-33.

Baronian, Jean-Baptiste. *"W* par Georges Perec." *Magazine Littéraire* Sept. 1975: 80.

Bellos, David. "Literary Quotation in Perec's *La Vie mode d'emploi." French Studies* XLI (1987): 181-93.

Bénabou, Marcel. "Autour d'une absence." *Quinzaine Littéraire* 1-15 May 1969: 9.

Berthier, Philippe. "Georges Perec, *W ou le souvenir d'enfance." Le Bulletin des lettres* 370 (1975): 255-56.

Bonnefoy, Claude. "Le Souvenir et le rêve." *Nouvelles Littéraires* 1-16 July 1973: 7.

Burgelin, Claude. "Perec et la Cruauté," *Cahiers Georges Perec,* I (1985): 31-52.

—————. *"W ou le souvenir d'enfance* de Georges Perec." *Temps modernes* 31.351 (1975): 568-71.

Buss, Robin. "Eleven Times Table." *Times Literary Supplement* 6 May 1977: 553.

Chalon, Jean. "Georges Perec, l'homme sans qui 'les choses' ne seraient pas ce qu'elles sont." *Le Figaro Littéraire* 25 Nov. 1965: 3.

Chalon, Jean and Jean Duvignaud. "Le Bonheur de la modernité." *Le Nouvel Observateur* 15 Dec. 1965: 32-33.

Clément, Catherine. "Auschwitz, ou la disparition." *L'Arc* 76 (1979): 87-90.

Cournot, Michel. *"La Poche Parmentier* de George Perec." *Le Monde* 22 Feb. 1974: 23.

Dällenbach, Lucien. *Le Récit spéculaire: Essai sur la mise en abîme.* Paris: Seuil, 1977.

David, Catherine. "La Chambre noire." *Le Nouvel Observateur* 10-16 Sept. 1973: 53.

Duvignaud, Jean. "Effet d'éloignement par rapport aux choses." *L'Arc* 76 (1979): 24.

—————. "Georges Perec, prix Renaudot 1965." *Le Nouvel Observateur* 24-30 Nov. 1965: 27.

Franju, Georges. "Au point mort de sa vie (sur 'Un Homme qui dort')." *Positif* 159 (1974): 57.

Galey, Matthieu. "Perec: des Mémoires en charpie." *L'Express* 28 July 1975: 16-17.

Gilbert, John. *"Un Homme qui dort,"* *Novel* 2.1 (1968): 94-96.

Godard, Colette. "Avant-première: Comment fonctionne la machine?" *Lettres françaises* 1323 (1970): 13.

Gollub, Judith. "Georges Perec et la littérature potentielle." *The French Review* XLV.6 (1972): 1100.

Goodman, Lanie. *"Un Cabinet d'amateur:* an Optical Disillusion." *SubStance* 29 (1981): 110.

Goulet, Alain. *"La Vie mode d'emploi,* archives en jeu." *Cahiers Georges Perec,* I (1985): 193-212.

Helmlé, Eugen. "Traduire *La Vie mode d'emploi." Littératures* 7 (1983): 99-103.

Kanters, Robert. "Les Choses et les mots." *Le Figaro Littéraire* 25 Nov. 1965: 5.

—————. "Aux écoutes de la nuit." *Figaro Littéraire* 17 Feb. 1966: 5.

Koster, Serge. "Quand le 'je' se change en nous." *Quinzaine Littéraire* 16-28 Feb. 1978: 7.

Labre, Chantal. *"Je me souviens." Esprit* II.3 (1978): 104.

Lalou, Etienne. "Un déserteur de l'histoire." *L'Express* 8 May 1967: 40.

—————. "320 pages sans la lettre E." *L'Express* 28 April 1969: 57.

Lascaut, Gilbert. "Les Nombres et un mode d'emploi." *L'Arc* 76 (1979): 44-49.

Leclerc, Annie. *"Les Choses,* un combat malheureux." *Les Temps modernes* 21: 235 (1965): 1135.

Lee, John. "Brise ma rime." *Littératures* 7 (1983): 11-20.

Magné, Bernard. "Cinquième Figure pour *La Vie mode d'emploi*." *Cahiers Georges Perec,* I (1985): 173-77.

―――――. "Lavis, mode d'emploi." *Cahiers Georges Perec,* I (1985): 232-46.

―――――. "Noms naufragés." *Littératures* 7 (1983): 141-50.

―――――. "Le Puzzle, mode d'emploi..." *Texte* I (1982): 84-86.

―――――. "Quelques problèmes de l'énonciation en régime fictionnel." *Actes du Colloque d'Albi.* Albi: Ecole Normale d'Albi (1982): 217-55.

Marissel, André. "Georges Perec: *La Boutique obscure*." *Esprit* 435 (1974): 909.

Mathews, Harry. "Le catalogue d'une vie." *Magazine Littéraire* March 1983: 16.

Mauriac, Claude. "Matière première onirique et production littéraire." *Figaro Littéraire* 18 Aug. 1973: II, 8.

Mauroux, Jean-Baptiste. "Georges Perec, *W ou le souvenir d'enfance*." *Quinzaine Littéraire* 1-15 June 1975: 11.

Misrahi, Robert. "*W,* un roman réflexif." *L'Arc* 76 (1979): 87-90.

Morrissette, Bruce. *Novel and Film: Essays in Two Genres.* Chicago: University of Chicago Press, 1985.

Motte, Warren. "Embellir les lettres." *Cahiers Georges Perec,* 1 (1985): 110-24.

―――――. *The Poetics of Experiment, A Study of the Works of Georges Perec.* Lexington: French Forum Publishers, 1984.

—————. "Georges Perec on the Grid," *The French Review* LVII.6 (1984): 820-32.

Oriol-Boyer, Claudette. "Le Voyage d'hiver." *Cahiers Georges Perec,* I (1985): 146-70.

Oulipo. *Atlas de littérature potentielle.* Paris: Gallimard, 1981.

—————. *La Bibliothèque oulipienne.* Geneva: Slatkine, 1981.

—————. *La Littérature Potentielle.* Paris: Gallimard, 1973.

Pawlikowska, Ewa. "Citation, prise d'écriture." *Cahiers Georges Perec,* I (1985): 213-31.

—————. "La Colle bleue de Gaspard Winckler." *Littératures* 7 (1983): 79-87.

—————. "Post-scriptum: figures de citation dans *La Vie mode d'emploi* de Georges Perec." *Texte en main* 6 (Winter 1986): 70-98.

Pedersen, John. *Perec ou les textes croisés.* Copenhagen: University of Copenhagen, 1985.

Peeters, Benoît. "Echafaudages." *Cahiers Georges Perec,* I (1985): 178-91.

Perec, Georges. *Alphabets.* Paris: Galilée, 1976.

—————. "Bibliographie sommaire." *L'Arc* 76 (1979): 96.

—————. *La Boutique obscure.* Paris: Denoël, 1973.

—————. *Un Cabinet d'amateur.* Paris: Balland, 1979.

—————. "Ce qu'il se passe quand il ne se passe rien." *Le Monde* 10 Feb. 1978: 17.

————. *Les Choses.* Paris: Les Lettres Nouvelles, 1965.

————. *La Clôture et autres poèmes.* Paris: Hachette, 1980.

————. *La Disparition.* Paris: Denoël, 1969.

————. "Emprunts à Flaubert." *L'Arc* 79 (1980): 49.

————. *Espèces d'espaces.* Paris: Galilée, 1974.

————. "L'Eternité." *Orange Export Ltd. 1969-1986.* Paris: Flammarion, 1986: 249-50.

————. "Fonctionnement du système nerveux dans la tête." *Cause Commune* 3 (1972): 42-55.

————. *Un Homme qui dort.* Paris: Denoël, "Les Lettres Nouvelles," 1967.

————. *Je me souviens.* Paris: Hachette, 1978.

————. *Konzertstück für Sprecher und Orchester.* Sarrebruck, 1972.

————. "Les Lieux d'une ruse." *Cause Commune,* I (1977): 77-88.

————. "Un livre pour jouer avec." *Le Monde* 29 September 1978: 18.

————. "La Maison des romans." *Magazine Littéraire* Oct. 1978: 35.

————. *Die Maschine.* Stuttgart: Reclam, 1972.

————. "Notes concernant les objets qui sont sur ma table de travail." *Nouvelles Littéraires* 26 Feb. 1976: 17.

————. "Notes sur ce que je cherche," *Le Figaro* 8 Dec. 1978: 28.

————. *Penser/Classer.* Paris: Hachette, 1985.

————. "Quatres figures pour *La Vie mode d"emploi.*" *L'Arc* 76 (1979): 51.

————. *Quel petit vélo à guidon chromé au fond de la cour?* Paris: Denoël, "Les Lettres Nouvelles," 1966.

————. "Des règles pour être libre." *Les Nouvelles Littéraires* 10 March 1977: 21.

————. *Les Revenentes.* Paris: Julliard, 1972.

————. *Série Noire.* Dir. Alain Corneau. Scenario by Alain Corneau and Georges Perec. Gaumont, 1979.

————. *Tagstimmen.* Sarrebruck, 1971.

————. "Tentative d'épuisement d'un lieu parisien." *Cause Commune* 1/75 (1975).

————. *Théâtre I.* Paris: Hachette, 1981.

————. *La Vie mode d'emploi.* Paris: Hachette, 1978.

————. "Le Voyage d'hiver." *Saisons.* Paris: Hachette, 1979.

————. *W ou le souvenir d'enfance.* Paris: Denoël, 1975.

Perec, Georges, and Robert Bober. *Récits d'Ellis Island.* Film. Institut national de l'audiovisuel, 1980.

————. *Récits d'Ellis Island.* Text. Paris: Sorbier, 1980.

Perec, Georges, and Alain Corneau. *Série Noire.* Filmscript. *L'Avant-Scène/Cinéma* 233 (1979).

Perec, Georges, and Jean-Marie Le Sidaner. "Entretien." *L'Arc* 76 (1979): 3-10.

Perec, Georges, and Gabriel Simony. "Entretien avec Georges Perec." *Jungle* 6 (1983): 74-89.

Peretz, Henri. *"Les Choses* (suite)." *Les Temps modernes* 21.235 (1965): 1138-39.

Pingaud, Bernard. "Ceci n'est pas un puzzle." *L'Arc* 76 (1979): 1.

—————. "L'Indifférence, passion méconnue." *Quinzaine Littéraire* 1-15 May 1967: 3.

Poirot-Delpech, Bertrand. " 'L'Augmentation' de Georges Perec." *Le Monde* 4 March 1970: 21.

Poirson, Alain. "Georges Perec. *W ou le souvenir d'enfance." Pensée* 187 (1976): 152.

Pétillon, Monique. "Les 'choses vues' de Georges Perec." *Le Monde* 10 Feb. 1978: 17.

Ribière, Mireille. "Alphabets." *Cahiers Georges Perec,* I (1985): 134-45.

—————. "Coup d'L." *Littératures* 7 (1983): 49-60.

Roche, Anne. "L'Auto(bio)graphie." *Cahiers Georges Perec,* I (1985): 65-80.

—————. "SouWenir d'enfance." *Magazine Littéraire* March 1983: 27.

Rocquet, Claude-Henri. "A la recherche de l'espace perdu." *Quinzaine Littéraire* 1-15 Dec. 1974: 24.

Schwartz, Paul J. "Georges Perec's *Un Cabinet d'amateur:* Portrait of the Artist as Iconoclast." *Perspectives on Contemporary Literature* 13 (1987): 11-17.

—————. "The Unifying Structures of Georges Perec's Suspended Memoirs." *International Fiction Review* Summer 1985: 71-73.

Slonim, Marc. "Sleeper." *The New York Times Book Review* 18 June 1967: 38.

Thompson, Jim. *A Hell of a Woman.* Berkeley: Creative Arts, 1954.

INDEX